Pandemic of Opportunism

America's Misuse of Medical Malpractice Litigation

Sarah L. Seymour-Winfield

Foreword by Erika Grushon, D.C.

...Let
not the dry dust that drinks
the black blood of citizens
through passions for revenge
and bloodshed for bloodshed
be given our state to prey upon.
Let them render grace for grace.
Let love be their common will...

Aeschylus
The Eumenides

**Braughler
Books**
braughlerbooks.com

937-58-BOOKS

Other works by the author –

Images Old and New:
The Judeo/Christian Mystical Tradition.

Now in the Archives of Thomas Merton
and the Library of the Harvard Divinity School.
Nominated for the Pulitzer Prize in 2011.

Second Edition Release scheduled for Summer 2016.

One Little Life:
A White Child and a Black Woman
Struggle Against Racism.

The childhood of Ms. Seymour-Winfield.

Grand Prize Winner for Non-Fiction:
Greyden Press Competition, 2014.

Dedicated to all physicians
who daily care for the sick, the injured, and the dying,
who despite the outcome of their treatments
sincerely strive to *do no harm.*

Foreword

In her latest book, *Pandemic of Opportunism*, Sarah Seymour-Winfield guides the reader along a remarkable journey from the darkness of her personal despair following a medical miscalculation onward toward the light of hope.

She paints a realistic and sensitive portrait of physician as a fallible human being, then offers a bird's eye view of all the emotional and psychological disruptions which inevitably follow medical error in the lives of the patient and family, as well as in the professional and private lives of the physician responsible and the larger medical complex. Her book offers a rare glimpse into the dueling perspectives between layman and attorney versus physician and attorney on both sides of this grueling and costly medical malpractice battle.

In our age when thousands of opportunistic lawsuits are causing the most sensitive and erudite physicians to question their continuance in their chosen profession, and when the deliberate omission of errors from medical records disables the profession from learning from its mistakes, this author invites our culture to pursue an alternate model to address medical error, one which though still reactive in nature and necessarily charged with powerful emotion, is nevertheless supportive of everyone involved, a new, responsible and merciful replacement for our current model which fuels the fury of vengeance and legal retaliation. This book is therefore a mediation, a space where anger and scrutiny are safely expressed, and where both physician and patient are simultaneously held to the highest ethical standard.

For all of us who inhabit the world's stage as either patient or medical professional, *Pandemic of Opportunism* leads us into a higher morality where this complex issue of medical error is based upon reciprocal understanding and affirmation rather than the desire to mutually and legally destroy.

I applaud this author who courageously revisited her painful trauma with strength, honesty, and eloquent style in order to create for all readers a vivid account of her experience, then apply it to teach transcendental compassion to all who have had, are having, or might of necessity be forced to endure tragedy in their futures. With the depth of empathy and compassion presented in this book, an augmented system of higher intellectual reconciliation is a viable possibility when negligible, serious, and sometimes fatal errors unfortunately occur.

Erika Grushon, D.C.

A Letter to the Reader

Two years ago, my husband died from complications of a disease which was dictated by his DNA to begin at age sixty. That same year, he was diagnosed. The nature of that disease was such that he could possibly have lived to old age and died from a condition totally unrelated, but because of the myriad complications, drug interactions, and various allergies which presented along the way, his lifespan extended for only one more decade.

During his final year, it completely escaped my notice that a two foot wasp nest swarmed with activity upon the side of our garage. I failed to notice that the exterior trim on the front of our home needed paint, so riveted was I on my husband and his obvious decline. The few hours I could spend away from his bedside, I devoted to getting legal papers in order, locating safety deposit box keys, and consulting with banks and our attorney to ensure that my transition from wife to widow would proceed as smoothly as possibly.

Despite the fact that my husband's death was anticipated, a mortal blow for which I myself was somewhat prepared, the prevailing expectation of this culture was that there was someone I could sue, that I would inevitably, almost of necessity, participate in holding someone responsible for his death. Though my husband had been inadvertently harmed by medical treatment during his final hours, a treatment which resulted in a shocking appearance which horrified me then and still haunts me to this day, it never crossed my mind to hold anyone responsible for a death which had been predetermined by his very genetic code.

I did not understand society's expectation of me until I began to study the escalating number of allegations of medical malpractice in the United States. I realized through my reading that during the months immediately following my husband's funeral, I progressed by means of personal reflection through layers of deepening understanding until I came to the conclusion so contrary to this nation's widespread belief in legalities and blame – in my case there indeed had been no cause to sue for malpractice.

This book is written for all those patients or loved ones of patients who realize that unintentional harm has been inflicted by a physician while sincerely striving to preserve life. It is my hope that they too will progress through the same months of agonized introspection as I did, coming at last to the conclusion that filing a claim would not only contribute to the intensifying malpractice crisis, but also find through a scrupulous examination of their own hearts that their contacting an attorney would be both mercenary and frivolous.

Sarah Seymour -Winfield

Pandemic of Opportunism

The Plaintiff's Grasp at Power

Part I

Pandemic of Opportunism

There is a tide in the affairs of men
Which, taken at the flood, leads on
to fortune...

William Shakespeare
Julius Caesar

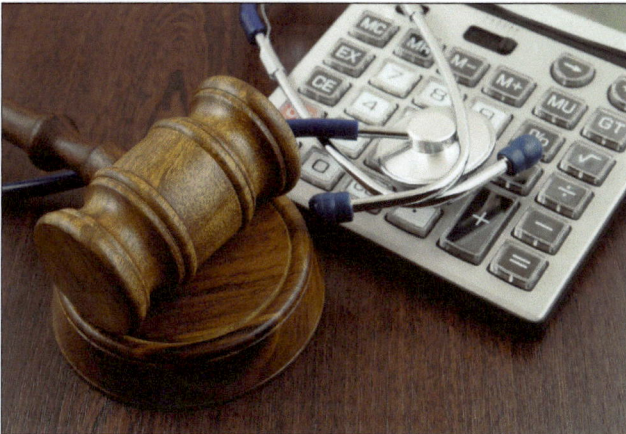

The Crisis

Electra:

Do you mean to judge or to exact justice?

Chorus:

Simply state one to kill those who killed.

Aeschylus
The Libation Bearers

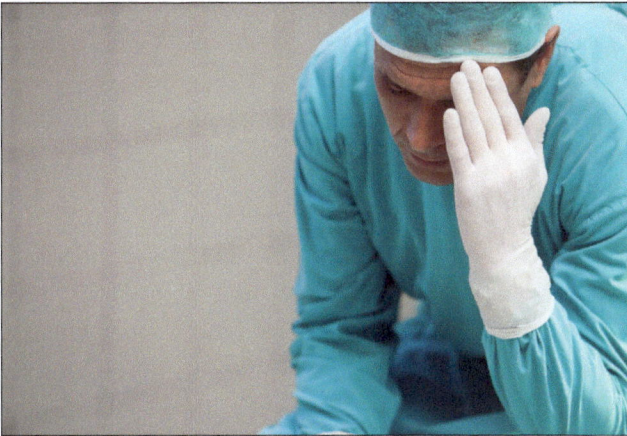

The Hippocratic Oath is one of the foundational documents of the Western World. Formulated in Greece during the fifth century BC by Hippocrates, the *Father of Medicine*, the Oath has expressed the guiding principles of the medical profession for twenty-five hundred years. Though alterations in the original text have been made over time, due to increased scientific knowledge and increased complexities of the art, the essence of the Oath has remained intact over the centuries, with some variation of the original included in most graduation ceremonies from medical schools. Doctors today swear in the presence of the Judeo/Christian God, just as physicians in the great age of Greece swore in the presence of Apollo the physician, Aesculapius the surgeon, and all the gods and goddesses, that throughout their careers they will uphold the highest ethical standards, will implement their knowledge in a God-fearing manner, and will maintain strict confidentiality between themselves and their patients. If knowledge of the patient or the patient's family is inadvertently acquired during the course of treatment, the doctor promises to refrain from all gossip, to keep that information as a sacred trust, secret within his own heart, since the patient's desire is that private information not be known to all. He promises to remember that his power of influence extends beyond his patient, that he is a member of a larger community, and that he has obligations to all his fellow human beings. The doctor assumes the awesome responsibility of treading the perilous border between life and death with profound meekness and utter humility, and with the strength of his innate personal dignity and continuous self-awareness to sincerely strive to promote life and to *do no harm*.

Young physicians joyfully embrace this covenant of moral and ethical perfection with full awareness that no matter how earnestly they strive for its realization within themselves and their careers, they are innately incapable of that very perfection which this noble Oath espouses, because as flawed human beings, they can and inevitably will make mistakes which result in greater suffering, tragic disability, or even worse, death to the patient. It is at this supreme crisis point in the career of the doctor, when his flawed humanity betrays his most honorable intentions, that the magnanimous precepts presented in this Oath are reversed by the general public, who are supported by national consensus that they to the emotionally devastated physician have every right to do harm.

Those who initiate unwarranted lawsuits against physicians for alleged medical malpractice with the dark and sinister hope of receiving settlements of hundreds of thousands if not millions of dollars, swear before the same Judeo/Christian God that they will uphold no ethical standards and display no inherent fear of God. They will delight when the confidentiality between patient and physician is destroyed by themselves and the lawsuit, will safeguard no private information about the doctor as a sacred trust, because their earnest desire is that knowledge of the physician's failings is broadcast by their own malicious gossip to be known by all. They are pleased that their power of worldly influence extends beyond the doctor because they are members of a larger community, and they cloak their opportunistic motives beneath the fraudulent belief that they also have an obligation to their fellow human beings. Plaintiffs assume the awesome responsibility of treading the perilous border between the success of the doctor and the death of his career with arrogance and aggression, and by forfeiting their own personal dignity and with a woeful lack of self-awareness, they actively strive to inflict upon the doctor and his profession deliberate harm.

The statistics are staggering. On average, 125,000 cases of alleged medical malpractice clog our legal system every day. Over 40% of all doctors will be sued, some multiple times. In high-risk specialties such as obstetrics, the rate is as high as 90%. Surgeons are particularly vulnerable, as are experts in emergency medicine who minute by minute make split-second decisions of life and death with little or no knowledge of their patient. One highly competent physician has been sued so many times, he is friendly with opposing counsel! Pennsylvania and Florida recently had so many alleged malpractice cases that many doctors abandoned these states. Clinics and Emergency Rooms have been forced to close because of the threat of litigation. A cartoon appeared of a courtroom where only the judge and two lawyers were present, because there was no one left to sue. This collective nationwide insanity is also a drain on the legal profession itself, as attorneys committed to providing equal justice for those in every stratum of intellectual ability in every stratum of income must now either defend or prosecute cases in a court of law which could easily be solved by the patient's simply going to another doctor or obtaining a second opinion.

The shocking number of yearly medical malpractice suits indicates that either medical schools are graduating thousands of students hopelessly unprepared for the rigors of their profession, or that this culture so rooted in greed and self-interest has discovered that the humanity and vulnerability of its physicians make them opportunistic targets from whom the public can exact enormous financial settlements, a legal form of vigilante vengeance which has been termed *Lottery Lawsuit.* Because of this sinister trend to prey upon our medical professionals who have dedicated their lives to aiding the sick, the injured, and the dying, upon whose compassion and expertise our very lives depend, doctors now realize that among their fellow physicians are only two kinds of doctors - those who are being sued, and those who are about to be sued. America's current indulgence in opportunistic lawsuits has become the newest societal pastime; the physician, however, upon whom this culture mercilessly preys, has become the newest form of *tragic hero.*

Aristotle defines the tragic hero as a man of elevated standing or high social rank, a man who is conspicuous in his society, but a man who is neither outstanding in virtue nor righteousness, neither is he distinguished for his wickedness. If a hero were so morally superior to us, the audience could not identify with his plight, and if he were so morally inferior to us, the tragic element of the play could not exist. He is differentiated from us solely by his noble position, not by a superiority of character. The tragic hero is very much like us, neither completely good nor completely bad, a creature with strengths and weaknesses, a man who possesses an inherent *hamartia,* which is *the ability to make a mistake in judgment.* The hero, like every member of his audience, is destined to make mistakes - to misjudge, to miscalculate, to misinterpret, to procrastinate, to rush, to underestimate, to overestimate, to discard as irrelevant what is most important, or to take as supremely important what should be ignored. Hundreds of possible flaws of character have the potential to lead inevitably to tragic consequences. It is the manifestation of the hero's flaw during the opening action of the drama and the consequences of that flaw manifesting over the course of the play which cause the hero to suffer far more than he deserves, and cause him and those around him to spiral down to ruin and possibly death.

The viewer experiences two primary emotions during the course of the tragedy – *pity* and *fear.* Because the hero is similar to us in his humanity, because we too have hundreds of possible flaws of character which could very well lead to tragedy in our own lives, we feel pity for him trapped within the web inexorably woven by his fatal flaw. We fear for him and those around him as the forces of destiny set into motion long before the play began, as well as by the singular weakness so apparent in his very nature, interweave, entangle, and tighten, the audience ever more deeply pitying the humanity of the hero and increasingly fearing his inevitable fate. The drama resembles a violent storm in which all the forces of the cosmos seem in direst combat to be interlocked. At the moment of maximum tension for both the performers and the audience as well, the insight of self-knowledge mightily dawns, the plot resolves, the web untangles, and the mind of the viewer, at the cost of the sufferings and perhaps the death of the hero, is brought to a deeper understanding of the essential nature of humanity. Through a *catharsis,* a *purgation* of the emotions of pity and fear, the human heart is plunged into a deeper compassion for our fellow man.

In the United States today, a deeper understanding of our essential nature and compassion for our fellow human beings should be present in abundance, because both in the medical community and in the non-medical laity, pity and fear abound. Doctors fear the very patients for whom they care, since there exists in every contemporary physician/patient relationship the ever-present danger of a lawsuit, a danger which becomes increasingly multiplexed when adult children of patients are involved. Doctors feel pity for members of their own profession who are struggling through the various levels of litigation. The laity who hear escalating reports that the profession is riddled with seemingly incompetent physicians, and who may pity friends or acquaintances whose medical procedures resulted in regrettable outcomes, are literally afraid to keep appointments, to submit to surgery, to submit to tests, or in a crisis situation to submit to the expertise of an unknown physician or a previously unknown hospital.

Though pity and fear are dominate in both opposing groups, the third essential of tragedy is conspicuously missing – the viewer's identification with the tragic hero, or in terms of this study, *the laymen's identification with the physician who has innocently committed human error,* who struggles to pursue his career of compassionate care of the sick, the injured, and the dying while suspecting he is laboring under the threat of a lawsuit, or who is overwhelmed by the rigors of the litigation process itself. Though books have been written recently outlining the various emotional trials every doctor must necessarily face when charged with medical negligence, these books, listed in the Bibliography, are written for physicians themselves to assure them that their feelings are not uniquely singular, but universally experienced by every doctor who is either threatened by or trapped within the throes of a lawsuit. The following section, however, will attempt to provide the essential Aristotelian element of tragedy which is conspicuously absent in the laity today - the emotional identification of all patients with their doctor as tragic hero.

In *Physician as Defendant,* the ever-deeper rungs of emotional hell through which every doctor necessarily passes who either suspects he soon will be or has actually been charged with alleged medical malpractice will be outlined for the laymen as they have been outlined for the professionals. Next, the processes of the *Patient or Loved One as Potential Plaintiff* will be presented, the potential plaintiff who, conscious of the pandemic of accusing doctors of their supposed inhumanity when they commit simple human error, is determined to **pause** after the crucial medical event, to pause to determine for herself, without consulting with an attorney, if filing a lawsuit for medical negligence is indeed warranted. It is my hope that the presentation of the emotional processes of both groups will enable the pity and fear so prevalent in each - the medical profession and those who have been unfortunately harmed by medical care – will result in deeper depths of empathy, deeper depths of compassion, and a deeper understanding of the innate goodness of the human heart.

The emotional processes of both physician as defendant and patient or loved one as potential plaintiff are based upon the primitive instinctual reflexes of fight, flight, and freeze, or tend and befriend. Every medical deviation from anticipated positive outcome is tinged with disappointment, discouragement, irritation, and varying depths of depression, but the drastic deviation of medical catastrophe, when the snow-globe of our very existence is violently shaken, when we stare vacantly at a psychic white wall in utter shock, is dominated by horror, a horror to which we instinctively react with primal feelings of endless contraction or expansion.

Those whose character is grounded in a firm sense of self in direct opposition to others may respond with the contraction of anger, lashing out at the physician and at nearby medical personnel, displaying intimidating body postures which accentuate her presence accompanied by a threatening tone of voice. The recipient of the medical error or the loved one who is cognizant of the error may pay no consideration to the consequences of her actions, and may forfeit as irrelevant her own personal dignity. Her behavior may be characterized by a frenzy of verbal violence, an incoherent jumping to conclusions, as well as an inability to process information, and poor listening skills. If her anger does not spontaneously subside, and she is left physically unrestrained, her intensity unfortunately may escalate to a rage which will be partially satiated only by the infliction of physical violence, or regrettably by the sight of blood. This is the *fight* reflex, rooted in primitive humanity, which in the devastating consequences of a medical catastrophe can still be witnessed today.

Those whose character is less firmly assertive may not be able to formulate a coherent response at all. She may simply faint or run away. She may lose her balance and display irregular patterns of breathing, hyperventilating or holding her breath. Most pitiably, she may express inappropriate emotion such as laughing in the face of disaster. She may stare wide-eyed in disbelief before retreating so far inward that she may appear to be in a catatonic state. This is the *flight* reflex which includes the *freeze* reflex, both enabling one to psychically hide, to either physically or mentally exit from an overwhelming situation.

Psychological studies on fight and flight were originally conducted using only men as the subjects. These findings were illustrated by using this proverbial example - that prehistoric man, confronted by a hungry lioness, would instinctively either attack the animal, or run from the animal, or freeze in a paralyzing dread. But when women were added as subjects to these studies, women experiencing overwhelm in situations of life and death, a new form of defense was discovered – the reflex of *tend and befriend.* Females have the responsibility of caring for their young. In a crisis situation, such as an approaching lioness, the instinct of the mother is not to fight, or to run, but to protect her young. This makes it an essential life-sustaining biological imperative for that mother to befriend the lioness.

These are the reflexive responses which will at various times be experienced both by the physician whose mistake created the crisis and by the patient or loved ones impacted by the error. Both groups, both sides of this medical catastrophe must necessarily contend with the primitive biological reflexes of fight, flight, freeze, and mercifully tend and befriend.

C8 80

The Physician as Defendant

Dangerous is the citizen's talk, with anger in it.

Aeschylus
Agamemnon

Depending upon the statute of limitations for filing a suit for medical malpractice in the particular state where the medical event occurred, the phase preceding the initiation of a lawsuit typically lasts from one to three years. For those physicians who are unaware that they have made a critical error, or that the patient or relatives of the patient are dissatisfied with the medical care provided or the results of that care, this phase has no impact upon the emotional life of the physician. Doctors simply continue their professional and personal lives. But for those physicians who realize that they have made an error which aggravated a patient's condition or contributed to a death, the anticipatory anxiety of possible litigation is ever-present. Since the mind cannot clearly distinguish between reality and fantasy, thinking they both are equally true, doctors dreading a lawsuit during this preliminary phase feel like they have already been sued.

Even before the patient may realize that the physician's treatment has caused harm, and even before the family may be aware that an error has occurred, the doctor who has misjudged, miscalculated, misinterpreted, underestimated, overestimated, or displayed any one of the innumerable flaws which qualify him as a potential tragic hero, who has exhibited any one of the innumerable imperfections which in every human being are inherently innate, is filled with fear of a lawsuit and also with guilt about his professional failure. He is filled with regret for his choices, filled too with sadness that his actions have already wrought or soon will bring devastating consequences. An error in judgment delivers a serious blow to one's self-esteem; one's personal pride is deeply shaken. One's innocent violation of the fundamental of every aspect of medicine, *do no harm*, inflicts deep humiliation and self-reproach.

During the months anticipating legal action, the doctor may exhibit classic symptoms of *Post-Traumatic Stress Disorder*, the psychic disorder which erupts when one has witnessed death or the infliction of serious injury to one's self or another, or been threatened with loss of integrity to one's self or others, a physical crisis which causes one to react with feelings of terror, horror, and helplessness. In cases when it is the physician himself who has inadvertently caused harm to the patient or hastened the patient's death, who has threatened the loss of integrity to the patient as well as to the doctor himself, the psychological upheaval and emotional disequilibrium which result from physician error may sear upon the doctor's mind the memory of the event. Day and night, he may view that crisis as one views an icon, a photographic still which, because of the threat of litigation, stubbornly refuses to slip into the past. That memory may prevent sleep, or disturb his sleep with nightmares, and may ultimately cause him to fear sleep itself. The memory of that crisis may preoccupy his thoughts during the day, and interfere with his private life with those he loves and with his professional life with his other patients. Not only is he worried about the possible legal repercussion of his past mistake, but he also lives in constant dread that he will most likely, almost of necessity, make in his professional future another error.

The loneliness and isolation of this period of self-incrimination is exacerbated by the latent potential of the litigation process. Everyone with whom the doctor has confided about his mistake in judgment during this preliminary phase, everyone to whom he has disclosed his professional lapse during this interval of profound stress, will most likely be issued a subpoena by opposing counsel to testify against the doctor using these confidences as damning evidence. Nurses, residents, interns, and other professionals who may have been in attendance when the crisis occurred, and who will in all likelihood be directly involved if a lawsuit is filed, may discharge the energy of their unique anxieties and fears onto the doctor as blame. Vulnerability is felt by everyone, but most especially by the doctor, whose personal failing is now publically known, and whose reputation is therefore out of his control. The physician and his colleagues may experience a state similar to a collective emotional heart attack, a collective professional pressure, the hearts of all freezing in overwhelming dread. During this preliminary period of collective anxiety and blame, it may be difficult for the doctor's consciousness of guilt not to deepen into shame that not only did one fail, but that one's very self is a failure. The remorse of the doctor and the fears of the group will force him alone into a fierce introspection, an intense psychic reclusion. Even before the patient or family of the patient may realize that something is wrong, the doctor is already suffering the pain and exquisite isolation of the witness stand.

For those doctors who for weeks, months, or even years, have anticipated a lawsuit, the issue of the *summons* may provide a moment's relief from the anticipatory anxieties of the preliminary phase. One's future is now known; the perfect storm has materialized; the battle for one's professional reputation has begun. But for those who were unaware that a lawsuit was a possibility, who may indeed have even forgotten the patient as well as her condition, the issue of the summons is a devastating frontal assault upon one's personal and professional integrity. One will undoubtedly feel anger at the injustice of a legal system which supports that those who have little or no knowledge of the complexities of medicine now possess the power to judge one who has invested hundreds of thousands of dollars in one's education, and painfully acquired hard-won lessons from years, even decades of emotional and psychological trials while learning one's art. Though anger, fear, and anxiety characterize this interval when the lawsuit is being formalized, the overwhelming feeling, the predominate emotional response in the physician will undoubtedly be *betrayal* - betrayal by the patient and betrayal by that patient's family - because the doctor whose life was committed to that patient's well-being and who indeed performed at his maximum ability to sustain that patient's very life is now labeled negligent, careless, and indifferent to human suffering. The cognitive dissonance between the physician's intent and the patient's or the family's response will most likely result in an appropriately targeted but largely silent rage.

Now the doctor, whose life has been selflessly devoted to others, must tend and befriend himself. His immune system and heart will undoubtedly be blasted. Though it is not typical for laymen to conceptualize that physicians themselves may have medical problems, it must be acknowledged that any medical condition from which the doctor suffered before the summons will be aggravated once the summons is received. These physical challenges may intensify the shame he experienced during the preliminary phase, because his needing the personal assistance of other physicians may be perceived as a reinforcement of his feelings of professional inadequacy. He may suffer from hypertension and hyper-reaction. Although the depression of the doctor may truly require psychological and possibly psychiatric care, he may be reluctant to seek such aid because of his fear that disclosure of his emotional needs may reflect upon his professional record. If he does begin to take anti-anxiety medication or antidepressants, he will necessarily require weeks if not months to adjust to their dosage and inevitable side effects. Because anxiety and sleeplessness will undoubtedly dominate his life and cloud his judgment, the physician now lives in constant dread that he will commit another error. Within the mental fog of sleep deprivation, he may imagine that inside the time frame necessary to resolve one lawsuit, he may make a different mistake which will begin another lawsuit filed by another patient.

As the physicality of the doctor is bombarded by stress and anxiety, he must necessarily learn the intricacies of the legal profession with which he had no previous experience. In preparation for the doctor's deposition, his malpractice attorney will unknowingly re-enact a scene with the physician which is portrayed with such gravity on exquisitely hand-painted Greek pottery – that of solemnly handing the doctor as contemporary performer the *acoustical tragic mask* of the hero. In Greek drama, all performers, including the tragic hero, wore masks during each performance, the mask with its small eyes and gaping mouth which is the identifying trademark of ancient theater. Masks were worn because the play was a sacred event dedicated to the god, Dionysus, but they also served a purely practical function. In the era before electricity, microphones, and sound equipment, the voice of each actor was required to project to listeners both near and far. Amphitheaters then were constructed in rows of seating which radiated upward and outward from the floor of the drama in a one hundred and eighty degree semicircle, a design which allowed for the greatest amplitude of the human voice. The wearing of the acoustical mask further assured that each word, spoken from the floor of the theater, would be conveyed with greatest clarity to the farthest row.   1

Tragic masks portrayed an intense, concentrated introversion. Lacking all subtleties of facial expression and all identifiable facial lines of unique character traits, the mask embodied nothing but *kenosis*, archetypal emptiness. The audience could not discern any identifiable character traits in the hero at the opening of his drama due to the utter absence of human expression in his mask. He was a character present yet paradoxically absent, near yet paradoxically far. Standing still at the opening of his drama, the hero appeared as nothing more than a statue, a psychic blank. It was only through his skillful conveyance of emotion through words and eventually through his actions which revealed to the audience his character's response to fate as well as his character's moral worth.

The acoustical mask also served an essential purpose for the performer himself. Greek tragedy includes inarticulate cries which defy linguistic expression, deep guttural moans and piercing shrieks which transcend the limits of concise verbal articulation. For example, one Greek word means the snorting of horses trapped in a fire, a word impossible to convey by any adequate verbal means other than a savage, inarticulate cry. These prehistoric subhuman sounds, these animalistic utterances which were encoded into our very DNA at the dawn of our species, would have resonated with frightening intensity within the confines of the mask, their horrifying reverberations transforming the actor almost instantly into the hero he personified. In preparing the doctor for his deposition, the attorney solemnly places into the hands of the physician the mask of the tragic hero. From now on through his trial, the doctor must convey a focused concentration, must delete from his

personality all subtleties of facial expression and all unique character traits. He must embody nothing but Archetypal Physician, empty to all but concise answers to the questions asked by the plaintiff's attorney.

The doctor's attorney also teaches his client the listening skills the defendant must exhibit during his deposition. This art of conscious and active listening was known in the ancient world of the Greeks as *akroasis*. The physician is instructed to answer only the specifics of each question in as few words as possible, since any extraneous information volunteered by the doctor could open a new line of inquiry which could be used against him during his trial. He is taught that a simply *'Yes'* or *'No'* or *'I don't know'* is adequate, though in his own defense, the doctor will undoubtedly long to elaborate. He is instructed how to navigate successfully through the manipulation of the plaintiff's attorney, how to avoid answering compound, leading, and hypothetical questions, and how to clarify the attorney's question down to the parameters which enable the doctor to answer the question with truth. The doctor is taught, among other skills, how to identify incorrect characterizations, oversimplifications, and inflammatory words designed to elicit an explosive response in the defendant. These listening skills, unfortunately, do not apply to any other relationship in the physician's world – not to his relationship with his wife, his children, his family, his friends, and not even to his relationship with his other patients. They are unique skills applicable only to the attorney/client relationship during the deposition and later during the trial.

During his **deposition**, the doctor faces opposing attorneys, a court reporter, and possibly a videographer. Because no judge is present, the questioning of the plaintiff's attorney proceeds without restraint. The Archetypal Physician must respond without emotional or psychological individualism. Wearing his mask, the doctor appears present yet paradoxically absent, near yet paradoxically far. Sitting still at the end of the table, he appears to be a statue. The attorney of the plaintiff, like the audience in the Greek theater, must discern the moral worth of the doctor solely through his skillful manner of speaking and his demeanor. The doctor at all times must be cooperative and articulate, taking every opportunity to convey that he is professionally competent. Though he must appear to be emotionally controlled and psychologically stable, the interior of his mask reverberates with the inarticulate cries of betrayal and the emotional spasms of his true nature, as he fights for his integrity, his reputation, his relationships, and his career. Wearing the mask of tragedy, he literally fights for his life as a doctor.

This facial facade of the hero necessarily impacts the entire life of the physician from now through his trial. His attorney will advise him against sharing the specifics of the case as well as his emotional turmoil with anyone except his wife, though if she would disclose any pertinent information to a friend in an attempt to acquire necessary emotional support for herself, the plaintiff could demand that the friend be brought in for questioning as well. If the doctor chooses to keep the litigation a secret even from his wife, the marriage may become strained with suspicion and doubt. Children will not understand the emotional turmoil and psychic preoccupation of their parents, and very young children will inevitably blame themselves for the obvious disruption in their family. Since the threat of litigation and the process itself can consume three to five years, a large percentage of a child's early life can be spent under the shadow of the lawsuit. Teachers and child care professionals may notice a sudden change in the child's behavior, and grade school teachers may report an inexplicable drop in academic ability. Children in the throes of puberty may feel that their father has shamed them, and teenagers may resent the additional burdens which will inevitably fall upon them as the litigation process proceeds. All this takes place as the doctor and his wife hope and pray that the plaintiff will mercifully drop the suit.

This same disturbing pattern will radiate outward from the family of the physician to all the other families involved, as the plaintiff and her attorney unsparingly pit doctor against doctor, nurse against doctor, hospital against doctor, and department against department, until the stable lives and livelihoods of everyone involved in the initial medical event are professionally disrupted and corrupted by bitterness and resentment. The litigation process also contaminates his office practice, because secretaries and nurses must manage innumerable phone calls from attorneys and cope with whatever additional work the lawsuit demands. Long-time patients will notice a change in the behavior of their physician, and wonder inevitably if they need to take their medical record somewhere else. The doctor himself may be reluctant to accept new cases of a more complex nature, and he may even become fearful and suspicious of the clients he has known and respected for years. Most tragically, he may refuse to accept patients who are insufficiently insured for fear that they be tempted to obtain a massive settlement through an unwarranted lawsuit.

As the doctor under litigation becomes increasingly isolated, his family and professional relationships in increasing disarray, and all his patients suffer the consequences of the arrogant self-assertion of one, it is perhaps inevitable that he will briefly contemplate or actually seek refuge in the psychic oblivion provided by alcohol and drug abuse. But the psychic refuge which is most tragic is that every year, four hundred physicians commit suicide. As medical schools each year celebrate the entrance of four hundred graduates who eagerly embrace their chosen profession with idealism and joy, four hundred others deliberately choose death rather than endure another moment of litigation. The scandalous suicide rate among competent doctors has marred this opening of this twenty-first century with an indelible stain, has engraved upon the national consciousness a statistic which should force this country to its spiritual knees with guilt and remorse. America's insatiable greed, sense of entitlement, and adamant refusal to accept that suffering and death are an integral part of life, cause the most erudite and sensitive physicians to reverse the fundamental tenet of the Hippocratic Oath; in a moment of utter worthlessness in the depths of black despair, the doctor to himself tragically inflicts fatal harm. Our nationwide response to such profundity of suffering should be nothing less than *eleos, compassionate grief, the pain felt at the sight of a destructive event which happens to someone who truly does not deserve it.*

If the deposition of the doctor took place in the darkest rung of Dante's *Inferno*, surely his trial is held upon the lake of ice at the bottom of Dante's Hell. Now enters the *Greek chorus,* twelve Athenian citizens who represent the viewpoint of the extended community, the perspective of the larger world. They, like the hero, wear the expressionless mask of tragedy, embody nothing but *kenosis*, visually convey an utter absence of human distinction, character, or charm. Their role is to observe the action as the drama unfolds, comment on the plot, and articulate to the audience what the hero cannot articulate for himself. Their *choral odes* elucidate the ancestry of the hero, and expound upon his relation to the gods and to his unfortunate flaw. In the era before changes of scenery and changes of set were conventional aspects of dramatic production, the chorus provided a glimpse into the past and the future by nuancing the broader history of the hero. The chorus was a window opened toward the larger world. Until Sophocles' *Antigone*, which exploded the chorus into twelve individuals who spoke their personal views directly to the king, the chorus of Aeschylus spoke as one voice, one unified consensus. A homogeneous group of indistinguishable commoners, the Greek chorus drew the audience into the drama by arousing its emotions and its investment in the hero's fate.

The contemporary **jury** embodies the ancient Greek chorus, twelve nameless commoners who represent the viewpoint of the extended community, the perspective of the larger world. They too wear the mask of tragedy which radiates toward the defendant nothing but an emotional void and an utter absence of charm. Their role is to observe the action of the courtroom drama as it unfolds to determine the character of the doctor as well as his professional competence, and to attempt to formalize in their own minds what the physician is not articulating for himself.

The **trial** is an extension and an amplification of the strain of the deposition, as exhibits of hospital records and test results which portray the devastating consequences of the doctor's error are presented by means of overhead projectors and oversized displays. The attorney of the plaintiff actively seeks to shock not only the eyes of the jury, but by extension, the eyes of the doctor's larger world. In this atmosphere of unbearable stress, the physician must remember every word of his deposition, because any discrepancies between his testimony during his trial and his testimony during his deposition will be used to discredit him. Like the tragic Greek hero, who initially appeared as nothing more than a statue, whose character was slowly revealed by his actions over the course of the play, it is not only the visual appearance of the doctor during his trial which must convince the jurors that he is emotionally stable, psychologically sound, and professionally competent. Still wearing his mask, it is also the *action* of the physician which will reveal his moral worth as he attempts to endure with superhuman patience and strength as opposing counsel actively seeks to destroy his reputation as well as his career. The jury watches and processes information as one homogeneous group until they are dismissed into the seclusion of the jury room, where the chorus of *Antigone* fragments from one into twelve independent perspectives before reuniting once again to deliver its verdict of innocence or guilt.

Even though most medical malpractice trials declare the doctor innocent, there is no sense of overwhelming elation when the verdict is pronounced. Hundreds of lives have been negatively impacted, professional relationships as well as families have been disrupted, children have spent years in emotionally disoriented homes, marriages have been strained, the doctor's own health has been challenged, and patients themselves have grown suspicious not only of the doctor who was tried, but of the profession as a whole. Illegitimate malpractice lawsuits conclude with no catharsis leading to a deeper understanding of our essential nature, except that we, at best are fundamentally self-centered and at worst, vindictively cruel. We experience no purgation which leads to deeper compassion, except that addressed to the individual physician who endured this *survival of the fittest*, this *trial by ordeal*. All this psychic upheaval resulted from one patient or loved one who could not accept the humanity of her doctor, who indulged in a lawsuit intrinsically lacking moral merit or medical worth. When readers are confronted with the dire consequences of physician error, these broader dimensions of a potential lawsuit must be responsibly addressed.

CB EO

The Patient or Loved One
as Potential Plaintiff

This matter is too great for mortal judge…

Aeschylus
The Furies

The patient or loved one of the patient who has experienced the horror of the medical catastrophe, who sincerely strives to stem the tide of unwarranted lawsuits against competent physicians will, like her physician, spend months in the disorientation of the preliminary stage. Most of that interval will be spent in a state of shock and profound disorientation. She may spend weeks, even months staring wide-eyed into space, her internal world dominated by an endless white wall of shock. Like her doctor, her immune system and heart will be blasted. She may suffer repeatedly from colds and flu and from chronic insomnia. Whatever medical issues she had before the crisis will be aggravated in the months immediately following the medical event. Some physical problems may arise because she simply forgets to take her prescription drugs. This sudden withdrawal from her medications will be compounded by blood sugar issues because she refuses to eat. Unfortunately, she may be reluctant to re-engage with her own or any other doctor at this time, so fresh is the trauma she has either experienced herself or witnessed in the one she loved. She may suffer from what is known as *the broken heart syndrome* – when the lower left ventricle swells out of proportion from a rush of adrenalin – which causes her heartbeat to be painful and irregular, sometimes a powerful sporadic thumping, and at other times rapid and faint. If sufficiently distorted, the heart may actually fail. If her shock was severe enough for her to entertain thoughts of suicide, she may view her heart's painful incoordination as a blessing, and simply wait to die.

**While in this state of shock,
it is imperative that she not contact an attorney.**

Do not assume that in one's frozen state of disbelief, one's choices are rational, intelligent, or grounded in either reality or fact. Never call an attorney from a Trauma Center or Emergency Room. Since it is assumed that family members will also be in a state of emotional and psychological disorientation, do not respond to any variation of the question, *"Are you planning to sue?"* Refuse to participate in the prevailing assumption that an unfortunate medical outcome, or the administration of a procedure which unintentionally harmed you or a loved one necessarily demands legal action.

Though an inadvertent medical error damages the physical, it is the invisible psychic wounds of the patient or loved one which most urgently need to be addressed. Since human beings instinctively reach out to others following a trauma, surround yourself as the injured patient, or you as the loved one caring for the patient, with the professionals who can most deeply care for the invisible wounds of your heart and soul. Psychologists who specialize in trauma and PTSD, clergy of your family's particular faith, and simply caring friends who are willing to sit silently with you in your state of dumb shock, are all invaluable in a time of medical crisis. During this interval when one's mental faculties are almost non-existent, while one is still locked in fight, flight, or freeze, it is imperative to resist the steadfast belief that one necessarily requires the intellect of an attorney. To substitute the mental processes of a lawyer when one's own mind is largely inactive both betrays one's very integrity as a conscious individual, and denies that one has the innate potential to resume one's objectivity once this period of shock has subsided. Even in states where the statute of limitations denies the filing of medical malpractice suits beyond one year after the medical event, the family still has time to navigate through several months of psychic disorientation before filing with conscious intent for apparent gross medical negligence if they themselves, without the input of an attorney, think their claim has rational merit. Delaying contact with the legal system allows the instinctive initial *reaction* of horror to subside into a conscious intelligent *response.*

During the anxiety of this preliminary phase, as the doctor and the hospital contact their own malpractice attorneys in anticipation of a lawsuit, documenting, scrutinizing, and scrutinizing again that same documentation, the action of the prospective plaintive must be to simply sit. Though this passivity necessarily includes the intense introspection of grief and loss, trauma, and possibly symptoms of PTSD, her behavior is fundamentally a conscious refusal to participate in society's belief that the legal profession is the first and not the last resort. Simply sit. Simply exist with your pain. Simply sit with your heartbreak. Tend and befriend yourself. Simply bear your personal tragedy surrounded by the assembly of caring individuals you require to cope with your traumatized heart and soul. For both you and the physician, feelings will inevitably well up in tsunamis of passion. Do not participate in their explosive nature, but rather observe them with the same dispassion as one observes clouds in the sky. If negative feelings threaten to overwhelm you, do not discharge their energy by writing letters of complaint. If a death is involved, include no derogatory insinuations in the obituary. Write no angry editorials for the local newspaper. Contribute no disparaging comments on the hospital website. Post nothing on the web, Facebook, or Twitter which would cast doubt upon the physician, hospital, or medical profession. Even if you would love to inquire, mortify your curiosity by not humiliating the doctor or the integrity of the hospital by requesting a copy of the records. Refuse in every way to intensify the collective anxiety inherent in this waiting. Direct that energy not outward, but inward. Simply stare at your personalized equivalent of my white wall, allowing the torrent of flakes in your snow-globe to settle. Regard your passivity as a respectful act of non-violent resistance.

Within the isolation and darkness of my early months of grief, during my own preliminary phase, when fair-weather friends abandoned me, when my phone stood largely silent, and my gmail went largely dead, my behavior, directed entirely inward, could very well have been described as temporary insanity. I wandered aimlessly around our house in my nightgown, mile after mile each day within our house, with my hair uncombed, my husband's ties and suspenders draped around my neck, his favorite stripped shirt tied around my shoulders, holding his hair brush in my hands and stroking his hair. A thousand times a day I saw the scene in the trauma ER, a scene frozen like an icon on my mind. Though my body wandered aimlessly, my consciousness at least one thousand times a day ran from the ER curtain to my husband, fell upon his chest, and screamed into his ear. A thousand times a day I ran to him. A thousand times a day I fell upon him and screamed. When I awoke during the night, my body went instantly rigid, because I was suddenly back in the ER hearing the indescribable sound of the metal rings as the doctor swept the curtain away. Many times I pondered suicide, how merciful it would be to be out of the ER. *'Not by violent bloody means,'* I thought, *'but instead by means more mild. I'm not eating anyway,'* I assured myself. *'I could simply starve to death.'* The snow in my globe seemed so hopelessly shaken that I imagined I would never again see clearly through that most violent of blizzards, never again possess the consciousness I had displayed before the doctor swept that curtain away.

Ten months into this most severe form of PTSD, two thoughts slowly surfaced which gave me enough distance from my own agony that I realized with a glimmer of hope that I was getting better. I realized with amazement that for nearly a year, the scene of the ER had actually served as my elemental strength. The trauma I assumed that I was bearing had actually been bearing me, giving my empty consciousness a strict focus of attention, mercifully providing a contemplative grounding in a whirl of undifferentiated white. Like a guide rope in a blizzard, the memory of the ER had paradoxically enabled me to survive. I would have gone insane *without* the constant replay of that memory. What I had previously thought of as temporary insanity was actually my coping strategy to help me survive a loss I did not think I could possibly sustain. It was with this first realization that the snow in my globe began to softly settle. My guide rope was leading me slowly...compassionately... away from the blinding white.

I also realized that the consciousness I assumed I had lost forever at my husband's death was reappearing when I began to empathize with my husband's attending physician, my myopic fixation no longer focused solely upon myself but expanding to the larger world.

I wondered that because that doctor himself had actually witnessed the consequences of his error as they occurred, and undoubtedly felt responsible for the outcome, was he also suffering from nightmares? Was he also staring at the icon of that medical disaster? While treating his other patients, was his mind drawn back to the same memory which continually haunted my own? A wider inclusive perspective was beginning to surface; wisdom was beginning to well up from a source deeper than my intellect. It was at the point of convergence of these two dawning realizations that the primitive reflexes of fight, flight, or freeze were finally being overpowered by my resurrecting ability of conscious, deductive thought. Primitive instinctual reactions could then distill into an integrated and mature response. Months of deliberate passivity and apparently aimless wandering had led to the possibility of meaningful, purposeful action.

This delay, this psychic pause, may lead the patient and her family to a conclusion totally unexpected from what would automatically be assumed in the restrictive logics of the legal arena, a pause which might very well enable everyone to understand and appreciate a larger perspective. I realized that in my situation, one attending physician would have been held accountable for a medical disaster, when in truth, he was forced into his decisions by a series of other decisions made by other medical professionals, choices in which he played no part. Like the tiny almost insignificant movements of tectonic plates, each choice, each decision outside his knowledge lead to a crisis in which the tragic slipping of plates could have resulted for him alone in a professional earthquake. These peripheral decisions extraneous to his actions might never be discussed during the process of litigation, where the administering of drugs, the timing of drugs, procedures, and the data recorded in the medical records alone are predominately argued. To have sued that doctor and his hospital as responsible for the disaster when I was fully aware of that larger picture, would have been an action which would have qualified me as opportunistic, unconscionable, and immoral.

If the patient or her family, after their own pause of deliberate passivity, choose to initiate a lawsuit because their particular case seems to have both medical and moral merit, the motives driving their choice are actually **more important** than the doctor's tragic mistake, because the power differential has been dramatically reversed: the error of the physician then was inadvertent, but the response of its recipient now is deliberate; the physician who once had power over the patient is now at the mercy of the patient herself. This sudden acquisition of dominance, especially in individuals or families whose pain and sudden loss make them susceptible to violence and rage, is very difficult for most to handle with any degree of either rational thought or emotional equanimity. The physician who once held the keys to life and death, who is pledged to inflict no harm upon the patient or the patient's family, is now confronted by those who have both the human potential and society's permission to destroy.

Absolute power corrupting absolutely will in all probability be graphically displayed in the motives of the plaintiff in unwarranted and frivolous lawsuits for medical malpractice. This power shift from innocent victim to savage aggressor is the fundamental of one of Eric Berne's most sadistic of the 'games people play,' *Now I've Got You, You Son of a Bitch.* When the dynamics of this deadly parlor game are applied to medical malpractice litigation, the doctor who at one time occupied the parental role is now the naughty child who is presumed guilty until proven innocent, and the patient who was once the innocent child is now the angry abusive parent. 2

This game requires only two participants – in this case the patient and her physician. The aim of the game is one's own justification for one's inherent rage which could very well have tormented the patient before the medical error occurred. Though it is true that no patient hopes for an adverse outcome, patients who indulge in this game take full advantage of such an outcome, venting in an opportunistic fury at the doctor through belligerent verbal exchanges and possibly physical violence before indulging in the drama of a lawsuit. The existential payoff of *Now I've Got You* is the proof that no doctor can be trusted, that all doctors are incompetent, a belief which could very well be fueling this pandemic of malpractice suits in the United States today. But the most tragic payoff is within the individual psyche of the patient herself - that she, exploding outward, no longer has to confront her own deficiencies, no longer has to deal with her own pain, no longer has to deal internally with the consequences of the physician's error. She and her society support that blame is rightly passed to the doctor, rightly placed upon his shoulders entirely. The sinister nature of *Now I've Got You* expands the patient's persecution of her physician from the salient medical event to his credentials, his experience, his age, his ethics, his attitude, his demeanor, his national background, his religious beliefs, his tone of voice, his facial expressions, his office practices, in short to everything about him which could possibly be employed toward his destruction. Whether this game is played in a doctor's office, a Trauma Center, a courtroom, a ball field, or in one's own backyard, *Now I've Got You* burns a wide swath of devastation.

This game is initiated by an opening provocation, which in the arena of medical malpractice is the physician's reception of the initial letter from the lawyer of the plaintiff. The defendant's emotional devastation and psychological destabilization, especially for those physicians who had no suspicion that the patient was contemplating legal action, will most likely arouse in the unconscious plaintiff a secret delight, that sinister demonic glee which is the source of the name of this destructive game. If the opening volley for the doctor is the reception of a letter, the opening volley for the plaintiff is simply picking up the phone. Readers sincerely attempting to refrain from filing an unwarranted suit as an act of non-violent resistance to society's expectation that human medical error necessitates that patients inflict upon their doctors deliberate harm, must simply reject all contact with the legal profession until one is no longer lodged in fight, flight, or freeze. Simply refrain from picking up the phone until clarity of mind resurrects. This shift in power, this conscious pause, and the absolute necessity of all potential plaintiffs to examine with scrupulous honesty their motives for seeking legal action are brilliantly portrayed in that masterful play of Reginald Rose *Twelve Angry Men*.

Twelve jurors are locked in a bleak, beastly hot jury room on a beastly hot afternoon to determine the fate of a nineteen year old man accused of mortally wounding the heart of his father with a switchblade. The evidence of two eye-witnesses appears to be so compelling that the youth will no doubt die from lethal injection. The guard assigned to the jury room door concludes that the defendant *'doesn't stand a chance.'* Though most of the jurors assume that the verdict of *guilty* will be established on the first ballot, the vote quite unexpectedly is eleven to one. Juror number eight has requested a pause. That's all, just a pause. He is described as –

a quiet, thoughtful, gentle man - a man who sees all sides of every question and constantly seeks the truth. He is a man of strength tempered with compassion. Above all, he is a man who wants justice to be done, and will fight to see that it is.   3

When his fellow jurors are annoyed at him for his calculated delay, he responds, *'(I)t's not so easy for me to raise my hand and send a boy off to die without talking about it first...I think maybe we owe him a few words. That's all.'*   4

During the pause...which lasts throughout the remainder of the play, jurors quite unwillingly expose their painful personal issues of transference and projection, unresolved issues with their own fathers and sons, as well as their various racisms and bigotries toward this disadvantaged youth born into a slum. But essentially each shakes the other from his fundamental existential indifference to the future fate of this young man.

During this merciless self-examination, the testimony of the two eye-witnesses is discredited. The woman, who wears bifocals, could not possibly have witnessed the murder because during that night, she was not wearing her glasses when the stabbing took place. Her testimony is discarded because she simply could not clearly see. The man's testimony is questioned as emotionally opportunistic by juror number nine, an elderly man, *defeated by life*, who mourns his aging.

'It's just that I looked at him for a very long time. The seam of his jacket was split under his arm. Did you notice that? He was a very old man with a torn jacket, and he carried two canes. I think I know him better than anyone here. This is a quiet, frightened, insignificant man who has been nothing all his life - who has never had recognition – his name in the newspapers. Nobody knows him after seventy-five years. This is a very sad thing. A man like this needs to be recognized – to be questioned, and listened to, and quoted just once. This is very important.' 5

As the deliberation continues, anxieties intensify and tempers flare as jurors, one by one, summon the courage to bare their ulterior motives buried for decades within their hearts with the same precision as the youth supposedly bared the heart of his father with a switchblade. After excruciating self-scrutiny of both their motives and their new awareness of the larger parameters of their projections, their unanimous verdict is reached after each juror achieves a flash of personal enlightenment before changing his original vote from *guilty* to *not guilty*.

During those bleak and empty months following my husband's death when I wandered aimlessly around the house in my nightgown, I was the court-appointed guard who locked myself inside my home for uninterrupted deliberation. I was the juror who requested the pause. I was the first discredited witness who, without her glasses, simply could not see. I too was the second eye-witness who desperately needed recognition of my loss, because I too was *frightened* and *insignificant*, unimportant and alone. During that most miserable time of my life, when my future loomed uncertain, all meaning lost, my dominate mood a massive depression, I would have welcomed nothing more than the authoritative voice of an attorney to say, *'Get some rest, Sarah. Sleep if you can. I'll take it from here.'* One phone call would have initiated the game *Now I've Got You*, would have shifted the power to me. One phone call would have ensured that I would be the center of attention for years, would have rescued me from my crippling isolation, and given me the energy and reason to stay alive without the man whom I had loved for half a century. One phone call, at no cost to me, would have eradicated my suicidal despair. I would have been *questioned, and listened to, and quoted just once.* That would have been *important* to me. I would have instantly received all the attention of a *victim*, an *innocent victim* for whom an attorney would eagerly *fight.*

Mercifully though, it was *not so easy for me to raise my hand* to call an attorney when the career of the doctor might be jeopardized, to call an attorney who would bring all the force of his noble profession against one physician who, simply because of his humanity and because of other professional choices in which he played no part, would be branded incompetent, negligent, and reckless. I was angered, incensed, not at the doctor, but at the system itself because I, the recent widow at the time of my greatest emotional fragility, now possessed the power to unleash such havoc against so many people, to tarnish or even destroy reputations, to pit doctor against doctor, nurses against doctor, hospital against doctor, department against department, to disrupt the lives and livelihoods of so many. I realized in outrage that I was no longer staring at the purity of my white wall; I was staring into the very face of evil. My God, such seductive power when I needed it the most! Such potential authority when I felt most weak! If I had initiated a lawsuit from these depths of my own vulnerability, striking at the heart of that physician's greatest vulnerability, I with exquisite self-awareness would have realized that I was committing the gravest of sins!

C8 80

The Divine Abyss

Thou, so far, we grope to grasp thee -
Thou, so near, we cannot clasp thee –

Christopher Pearse Cranch
So far, so near

It is far easier for human beings to bear the strength of anger than to bear such helplessness when faced with the devastating consequences of medical error. It is far easier to bear the power of outrage than to feel the depths of such profound vulnerability in the presence of that overpowering force of destiny, that ruthless and relentless power of tragic fate, which reigns supreme far beyond both the conscious will and expertise of the physician as well as far beyond the most earnest desire and conscious control of one's very self. This eternally omnipotent irresistible force, which is the heart and soul of every tragedy, was labeled by the ancient Greeks as *Tyche,* meaning *Necessity.*

Greek tragedy is based upon this fundamental principle of Necessity, that force deliberately set in methodically measured motion before the curtain of the stage is raised. Necessity is destiny's thunderous dictate which predates the spectacle of the drama itself, because its fate has echoed throughout the universe since before creation. The remainder of the play is simply the viewer's own participation in the distant reverberation of that echo. Audiences watch in horror as tragic heroes writhe and twist and painfully suffer within the confines of their destiny as they hear the stubborn resilience of that sound which issued forth long ago specifically for them. We suffer pity and fear for Oedipus who, desperately attempting to avoid the fulfillment of the oracle which prophesied that he will kill his father and marry his mother, flees to another city where he, nevertheless, kills his father and marries his mother. Antigone's force of destiny was predetermined since before the dawn of time, since the laws which she adamantly upholds are older than Zeus. When Creon, the king, demands to know if she buried her brother despite her knowledge that the law stated specifically that the body of her slain brother, the traitor of the state, remain unburied, she replies –

Yes, I did. Because it's your law,
Not the law of god. Natural justice,
Which is of all times and places, numinous,
Not material, a quality of Zeus,
Not of kings, recognizes no such law.
You are merely a man, mortal,
Like me and laws that you enact
Cannot overturn ancient moralities
Or common human decency.
They speak the language of eternity,
Are not written down, and never change.
They are for today, yesterday, and all time.
No one understands where they came from,
But everyone recognizes their force:
And no man's arrogance or power
Can make me disobey them. I would rather
Suffer the disapproval and punishment
Of men, than dishonor such ancient truths.

6

With that statement, so dignified and self-assured, so rooted in ancient inarticulate moralities, her fate is sealed; her destiny must of necessity be fulfilled. Her tragic future is now known.

Some who in a state of shock experience the devastating consequences of medical error, who suffer at the hands of one who unwittingly inflicted harm, will most likely cry out in self-righteous outrage at the injustice of receiving death from one vowed to preserve life. They will writhe and twist within the confines of their own personal agony, suffering their unique pain like the greatest of the tragic heroes, shouting to the heavens that their fated destiny was not only a product of medical negligence, but that it undoubtedly arose from criminal intent! These unfortunates may remain locked in the vengeful grip of this childish earthly mindset forever, venting the lowest dregs of their adolescent rage upon all the world by perpetuating the medical malpractice crisis so evident today.

For others, it is the dread of the inescapable force of destiny driving all human existence, the terror of this capricious power beyond all human containment which is unrestricted, unmanageable, and ungovernable, which causes the instinctive reactions of fight and flight to reverse their polarities, because the *fight reaction toward* the attending physician who committed the innocent mistake is actually the *flight reaction away* from the presence of the Holy, away from the overwhelming and terrible power beyond the ability of one's own self and the ability of the doctor to manipulate, a force of Holiness which reduces the physician, the patient, and the family of the patient to the nothingness of dust and ashes.

The *Holy*, or *Holiness* are terms usually particular to the field of religion, though they can extend into the realms of the philosophical and into ethics. The Holy implies the ineffable, the inexpressible, the unspeakable, the Holy which eludes every conceptual apprehension. In the contemporary world, the Holy implies all that is good, completely good, nothing but good, the absolute moral perfection, the consummation of the moral. It implies a superabundance of its essence, of its goodness, an *overplus* of itself. However, in Hebrew, Greek, Latin, and other Semitic languages, the original meaning of the Holy was solely this overplus without any other conceptual distinction, an overplus of itself. Gradually this conception of overplus acquired the attribute of goodness as we currently understand moral perfection, but originally the Holy meant only the extreme of the ineffably sublime. 7

The violent intrusion of the overplus of this living supernatural force whose latent potential can reverse the primitive reactions rooted in our very DNA, this horror which, in a medical catastrophe, erupts into our lives from a dimension beyond our comprehension, is the presence of *The Wholly Other, The Mysterium Tremendum*, whose awful terrifying power causes us to spontaneously shudder, to tremble inwardly to our innermost core, causes the hair on our extremities to stand on end, our very flesh to crawl, chills the hot blood in our veins to run suddenly cold, and forces physician, patient, and family to fall prostrate in utter humiliation. The Mysterium Tremendum is the horrific *awful grace of God* which mercilessly, pitilessly reveals humanity's frailty before and vulnerability to the power dictated by fate, a *horror (which) slashes through life's surfaces and exposes the heart of our condition. It cuts through all of our comforts, from the obvious to the sublime, and unveils our rootlessness.* The inherent nature of the Mysterium Tremendum mercilessly suspends us over its infinite Divine Abyss, swallowing up the darkness of our meager understanding with the Darkness of Itself. The Mysterium Tremendum is horrifying because it is essential, intrinsically a sublime nullity, an infinity of *Nothing,* the mystic Void *which eludes all the thoughts ever conceived in any language, soars beyond all our proud, self-stroking intellectual knowings, falls like an eerie blindness upon every spiritual retina, chills all the feelings humanity has ever felt. Nothing stands a dark and frozen Himalayan contradiction to life's sun and all its warmth, yet this stark and barren Nothing is the Alone who dwelt alone before all other created alones.* This Nothing, this Alone, this Infinite Abyss is a terror which engulfs all in its dimensionless immensity. The Mysterious Tremendum is a horror which *suspends, it does not ground.* A medical tragedy not only exposes us, perhaps for the first time, to the galvanic majesty of the Judeo/Christian God whose essence far exceeds the meager depictions in creeds, contemporary religious practices, dogmas, and art, but also violently interjects into the doctor/patient relationship and into the compassionate intent of the medical profession as a whole the horror of the Dionysian.   8

Dionysus was the god of intoxicating mystical ecstasy but also of unspeakable pain and savage persecution. Born of a mortal woman but fathered by Zeus, Dionysus lived as an immortal but suffered as a man. At his conception, his mortality was infused with divinity, a paradoxical blend which did not negate his humanity, but rather magnified his ability to suffer, because this mortal god, by his unique parentage, was doomed to feel the agonies of the human species. All his worshippers who passionately loved and adored him, of necessity shared his tragic fate. It was within the cult of Dionysus that Greek tragedy was formulated, within his sanctuaries that tragic plays were performed as heroes, whose noble position in society mimic the stature of the god, but whose one mortal failing drives them relentlessly to suffering and even unto death.

Dionysus burst into the consciousness of the ancient Greeks from a foreign land, *from abroad and as something alien,* intruded into the Olympian pantheon as a stranger. Everything about him was disturbing and disquieting, an overplus of the violent. His very conception and birth embodied the horrific *fraternal confluence of life and death.* Only weeks into her pregnancy, his mother was incinerated when she beheld the full transcendental majesty of Dionysus' father, but Zeus rescued his son from the mother's ashes then, sewing the embryo into his own thigh, the god of all gods gestated his son himself. In an alternate myth, the child Dionysus was torn limb from limb and devoured, all but his heart which his own mother ingested, regenerating her son once again. Tragic death and indestructible life are inextricably welded in his nature, a severity of hydrogen bonding which displays both the life-sustaining as well as the death-dealing potential locked within the core of every atom, a god who served as a psychic premonition of the Judeo/Christian Mysterium Tremendum. This god is appropriately depicted accompanied by the bestial wildness of panthers, a god who incarnates the crazed unpredictability of his father's lightning bolt. In striking contrast to his half-brother, Apollo, who embodied all the artistry, order, and lyric grace of ancient Greece, Dionysus brought the power of the impetuous, the unmanageable, the ungovernable, the unbridled. He shattered all elegance of law and moral stability, *mocked all human order.* Dionysian energy today is Dylan Thomas' *force that through the green fuse drives the flower,* Emily Dickinson's *Panther in the Glove,* the subtle tectonic shift which prompts a volcanic eruption, the meager spark which sets a mighty forest ablaze, the unfathomable strength of a dandelion which forces its humble way through concrete. Among the Greek immortals who lived in consummate majesty above the clouds in a realm of undifferentiated ethereal bliss, Dionysus was *l'enfant terrible* of the pantheon. The most striking image of his singular identity as a mortal god is the *mask.*   9

Paintings from the ancient world show the mask of Dionysus suspended on wooden columns or positioned in grottos, portrayals of the god around which his worshippers perform their various acts of cultic worship. These masks were sometimes life-size and made of lightweight materials, but sometimes they were of colossal stature and made of marble. It is this portrayal of the god which contained in its very lifelessness the inherent dominance of the transcendental, because the mask of Dionysus, which is inherently only a flat inert surface, embodies nothing but the essence of spiritual encounter from which the viewer cannot escape. It provides no artistic subtlety in which humanity can psychically hide. The lifeless orbs of the god's monstrous vacant eyes stare directly and mercilessly at the viewer, shattering his composure with their penetrating stare, violently assaulting his entire being with the urgency of the Divine Abyss. The paradoxical enigmas of the raw and ruthless life force versus the indiscriminate brutality of destruction and death are inherent in its very gaze. The mask of this god who first appeared as a stranger, is a simultaneous manifestation of a reality both shockingly near yet unapproachably distant, *of antithesis and paradox, of immediate presence and complete remoteness.* The mask of Dionysus is a void, a mighty nothing, an eternal reminder that the transcendent is that mysterious and terrifying realm of what to us is Wholly Other. 10

It is the energy of the Dionysian which erupts as gigantic reality in the aftermath of medical error, as the doctor embodies the *antithesis and paradox* that the physician of life is now an instrument of death. He is now to us a stranger, an *alien*, one who embodies the *fraternal confluence of life and death* in a maddening ambiguity which *mock(s) all human order*, shatters our composure, imposes the fresh chaos of the uncontrollable, the ungovernable, the unmanageable onto our orderly existence, destroys every grounding, and suspends us over an infinite Abyss from which we cannot escape. In a medical catastrophe, the mutual confrontation of the patient, family, and physician with the Dionysian element is an unmistakable, unavoidable reality. It is to this explosion of primeval energy that the potential plaintiff must one day inevitably respond.

ᘓ ᘔ

The Trial of the Potential Plaintiff

...tangled in the nets of Justice.

Aeschylus
Agamemnon

Every patient or loved one who has suffered the consequences of physician error, who has stumbled through the darkness of the preliminary stage, is inevitably put on trial by her own conscience to finally declare her intention and to pronounce her choice. At this time when her shock has spontaneously subsided, when her strength has given way to the utter exhaustion of inevitable grief, when she perhaps for the first time feels the full impact of her loss, she must now demand of herself a judgment. She must of necessity make her choice – whether or not she will sue. Her physician faced this isolation at the beginning of his own preliminary stage when his fear of a lawsuit was interpreted by his mind that he had already been summoned. Now it is she at the completion of her preliminary stage who is subjected to the exquisite pain and existential isolation of the witness stand.

Under the scrutiny of her internal judge and the piercing eyes of the chorus of jurors who represent her world, opposing views within her own conscience argue every definition which she has ever held as absolute truth. Definitions of *appropriate compensation* are immediately dismissed as juvenile and irrelevant, but every aspect of the term *justice* is scrutinized to a minute degree. She listens as both internal attorneys argue if the physician is a *skilled technician,* or if indeed every physician is *a god.* She hears strong arguments against a doctor who *makes a patient worse,* and in the background of the din the term *Hippocratic Oath* surfaces repeatedly. She hears shouts of *catastrophic disability,* and *unspeakable damage* to which his attorney can offer no valid objection, but she hears that same attorney, in the doctor's defense, reiterate again and again *appropriate standard of care.* As efforts to convince intensify, and shouts erupt more frequently of *Objection! Overruled! Sustained!,* she paradoxically grows increasingly bored. Though she may be a writer whose very life is dominated by language and the complexities of thought, she grows increasingly bored. As the drama in her own mind now proceeds in mercifully muffled tones without her active involvement, the wisdom of that spiritual giant, Søren Kierkegaard, becomes to her increasingly clear: *Oh, the sins of passion and of the heart – how much nearer to salvation than the sins of reason!* 11

Her boredom is based upon one elemental flaw in the reasoning of both attorneys, one fundamental inaccuracy which makes the entire case inadmissible in any court of law – *that though the physician himself was the singular inflictor of the wound, she and her family alone were the only ones who received it.* Now there dimly dawns in her consciousness the inclusive truth that it is not she and her family alone who suffer the tragedy of medical error, that it is not the patient and family alone who bear the wielded wound. It is they and the physician together *whom the fates have mark'd / To bear the extremity of dire mishap!* Doctor, patient, and family now hover over the same Divine Abyss equally swallowed up in the Mysterium Tremendum. All have been equally and innocently impacted by *the awful grace of God.* 12

Those so fortunate to experience this stunning moment of enlightenment will meekly acknowledge that doctor, patient, and family were fated to trespass the same outermost border of human consciousness. Their souls silently scream with Tennyson, *O living will that shalt endure / When all that seems shall suffer shock.* They will suddenly understand the depths of the wisdom of Marcus Antonius, *Whatever may happen to thee, it was prepared for thee from all eternity; and the implication of causes was, from eternity, spinning the thread of thy being, and of that which is incident to it.* They grasp the concept of Robert Browning, *But here is the finger of God,* knowing to the depths of their being that through the disaster of the medical mistake *eternity affirms the conception of an hour.* These so fortunate few are now unprotected and utterly vulnerable, because they are strangers in this *most uninhabitable headlands of the divine "know thyself."* They now breathe the rarified air of eternity at that dizzying stratospheric height *where the psychology of Man mingles with the psychology of God.* 13

Her mind stops. The harsh lights of her bold self-assertion and self-consciousness suddenly dim. All struts of personal pride and pompous displays of personal power are abruptly obsolete. She can no longer rely upon their artificial strengths, because she no longer possesses any intellectual facility to support them. She possesses no dexterity for defensive leaps into the abstracts of philosophy, and the bold assertions of theology she simply forgets. In this outermost frontier of the mind, she is now an alien even to herself.

In that dim region far below conscious thought, she faintly perceives as irrefutable truth what she has previously known only as logic – that she herself is an amalgam of the finite and the infinite, that her eternal destiny is to embody with grace this *tension between incompatibles.* It is in bearing the consequences of the tragic that she will display her moral worth, will be brought to a deeper intimacy with her inmost self. This is the *high trial of the finite,* where she solemnly swears that her finite will *accept the judgment of the infinite.* She, like Antigone, vows to live transparent to *the language of eternity,* to personify to the full extent of her capacity divine not human love. She vows to submit to the laws *of natural justice,* those *ancient moralities* of compassion and *common human decency* which *are not written down and never change,* which are *for today, yesterday and all time.* No societal pressure can force her to compromise her integrity by initiating a lawsuit which she knows has no rational or moral merit, because she herself *would rather suffer the disapproval and punishment of men than dishonor such ancient truths.* She chooses not to sue. [14]

She has arrived at this spiritual perception of herself and her life through the horror of the tragic. It was the glimpse of the horror in whose presence she screamed which has brought her to this depth of realization, her witness of the tragic which has plunged her into a deeper understanding of her own essential nature and a deeper compassion for her fellow man. As all of humanity hovers over this Abyss of Divine Love, for anyone to arrogantly place blame solely in the hands of the physician, asserting as truth that whatever medical outcome contrary to her selfish personal preference is intrinsically wrong, is not only believing an immature assumption based upon pleasure-seeking and illusion, but is actually committing a contemporary form of blasphemy.

During the month when I began to empathize with that attending physician and expand my horizons beyond my own pain, I drove one evening to that same hospital, parked on the street near the ambulance entrance, and remaining in my car, studied the doors to the trauma ER. I was shocked to see that they were the size of ordinary sliding doors, because the morning of my husband's final emergency, those doors in my mind seemed to soar upward at least thirty feet. I had perceived them then as the gates of Milton's Hell, which *On a sudden open fly / With impetuous recoil and jarring sound /...and on their hinges grate / Harsh thunder, that the lowest bottom shook / Of Erebus.* Contemporary psychology would explain that I was so deep into shock that my sense perception was hopelessly altered, that my ability to orient myself in space and time through incoming visual and auditory data was fractured because of my panic about my husband's approaching death. But I know now that my senses that morning were exploding in a desperate attempt to accommodate the Dionysian presence of the Mysterium Tremendum. The awfulness of God before my mind then loomed so colossal that its violent manifestation demanded an equally violent response in me. Such vehemence has no parallel in the reaction to any phenomenon in this purely physical world. It bears witness *to a completely new function of experience and standard of valuation, only belonging to the spirit of Man.* Such explosive expansion is possible solely because we are ensouled beings who, captured from eternity, must live for a time within the confines of this mortal world. But that dreadful morning, I marveled, Spirit called to spirit. *Deep call(ed) to deep.* My response was instantaneous.   15

As I sat in my car studying those doors appearing of such pitiful dimension in the twilight, I realized that the world would now witness a recent widow, who once nearly drowned in grief, mercifully return to her senses, mercifully ground herself once again in the ordinary phenomena of this natural world. But to that realization, I responded with deep regret that the horror and majesty of that morning were fading. To regain the placidity of this world I must lose the Dionysian

SARAH L. SEYMOUR-WINFIELD

extremes of the other. The Mysterium Tremendum was retreating to a more comfortable distance. The Wholly Other was shrinking itself to a proportion which I could without effort bear. The frightful immediacy of the transcendental was growing more and more faint. I sat in my car and wept.

Whatever facts which in a courtroom are passionately pleaded, are always less than the mystical essential which the doctor and his patient inherently know – they both possess a *doubleness of nature*. They both are mysterious amalgams of the mortal and the divine. They both are creatures of spirit locked for a moment within the confines of the material as well as in the vice of their mutual catastrophe while acknowledging through tears of agony that they both are *citizen(s) of somewhere else*.   16

CȘ ȘO

Toward a New Ontological Security

The first function of a mythology
is to reconcile waking consciousness
to the mysterium tremendum...

Joseph Campbell
The Masks of God

(When) beliefs no longer universally held (are) universally enforced...the result (is) a dissociation of professed from actual existence and...consequent spiritual disaster...For those in whom a local mythology still works, there is an experience both of accord with the social order, and of harmony with the universe...For those, however, in whom the authorized signs no longer work...there flows inevitably a sense...of dissociation from the local social nexus.

17

Shortly before the American Civil War, a little boy was dying. His aging doctor piled him high with quilts and comforters, stoked the bedroom fireplace to a roar, sealed the bedroom window against the winter winds, and violently snapped together the drapes. After an hour in stifling temperatures, the child was closer to death. In desperation, the aging physician summoned his young student who doused the fire in the fireplace, tore all coverings off the bed, violently snapped apart the drapes, shattered the glass in the window with a chair, and packed the boy in ice. After an hour in frigid temperatures, the child died.

Neither physician was responsible for the boy's death, because we understand. Neither was guilty of malpractice. That we intuitively know. We understand because the drastically different dichotomies in treatment harmonize with our dualistic patterns of thought. We also understand that the affirmation of the aging doctor was ultimately not in contradiction to the affirmation of the younger. The death of the boy occurred because the death of the boy was destined to occur. That we understand. Even we laymen understand that disease proceeds through a relentless progression which sometimes can be halted by medical intervention, but sometimes unfortunately cannot. Even we laymen understand that the body is a complex and interrelated system, and that despite the very best of medical care and intention, that system can and often does progressively fail. Though the outcome will be in direct opposition to our personal will and violate our most earnest desire, plunge us into grief and even into the depths of suicidal despair, the outcome nevertheless is within our comprehension. It follows physical laws which we can grasp, laws which we can fathom, because these foundational principles are consistent with the nature of cause and effect within our minds.

But when a surgeon unknowingly nicks the bowel and causes fatal infection, when a minor error necessitates the amputation of one or more limbs, when an innocent miscalculation destroys a patient's brain, when the physician of life becomes unwittingly an instrument of death, our collective consciousness reels and wobbles and ultimately staggers to *th'extreme verge* of its understanding, because we find ourselves in the stratosphere far above discursive thought where all things sensible and intellectual are made null and void, where our juvenile dichotomies cannot be supported or sustained, where all religions fail as well as their symbolic expressions, *where the pure, absolute, and immutable mysteries of theology are veiled.* Psychically we fall flat; physician, patient, and family fall flat. Stranded in that strange and foreign frontier above *the topmost altitudes of holy things, plunged into the Darkness where truly dwells...the ONE Who is beyond all...we pass not merely into brevity of speech, but even into absolute silence, of thoughts as well as of words.* The very fiber of our being groans from the depths of Poverty of Spirit, 'Life is but life; death is but death. Beyond that ultimate simplicity, I know nothing.' Within this Darkness of Unknowing, where *all perfection of understanding is excluded,* the discussion of blame, accountability, lawsuits, and money is a sacrilege. 18

This is the clash, the mythological disharmony between my personal medical beliefs and the expectations of this culture which I experienced after my husband died. Because a split-second decision had been made by a physician during my husband's final crisis, an error occurred which aggravated his already fatal condition, resulting in a facial distortion which truly horrified both my children and me. When the curtain was withdrawn and I saw my husband's face for the first time, I ran to him, fell upon his chest, and screamed into his ear. His countenance had slashed through the surface of my life, cut through all my comforts. The horror of his appearance unveiled what was *expected* to be my rootlessness. It was my response to that horror which placed me in opposition to this cannibalistic culture so grounded in every form of entitlement, in which every doctor who deviates from perfection is *supposedly* worthy of being publically destroyed. Though I truly did feel horror at that moment, and still remember the experience of that horror to this very day, I did not at that time feel rootless, because my fundamental belief is that no physician, however scientifically erudite, is God. God alone is God. Though that doctor rightfully and nobly voted for my husband's life, God had voted for my husband's death. In response to that stalemate, in response to that tie, my deciding vote was for mercy.

During the era when the Father of Medicine was formulating his Hippocratic Oath, the ancient Greeks within their democracy abolished the vindictive form of justice so prevalent today, evidenced in the mercenary lawsuit for medical malpractice in which I could have consciously indulged. In his literary masterpiece, *The Eumenides*, the great tragedian, Aeschylus, dramatizes the moment when blood vengeance, embodied by the *Furies*, transforms into a more enlightened response. The young man, Orestes, is clearly guilty of murdering his mother in cold blood by stabbing her through her heart with a sword. The god, Apollo, who inspired this act of matricide, declares him innocent. Nevertheless, Orestes is hounded and tortured mercilessly with guilt by those ancient goddesses, the Furies, whose archaic strictness demands the cruelty inherent in *"Eye for eye, and tooth for tooth."* Orestes flees for refuge into the legal arena where an impartial jury listens to his testimony, considers all extenuating circumstances, examines his motivations, and most significant for the purposes of this study, imagines the potential ramifications of its decision. The goddess, Athena, daughter of Zeus, orders the jurors to *consult their conscience, and cast their vote.* The chorus adds, *Also remember the primal laws of the earth.* Athena proclaims –

Citizens of Athens!
This is the first case of homicide
To be tried in the court I have established.
This court is yours. From today every homicide
Shall be tried before this jury
Of twelve Athenians.
And this is where you shall sit, on the hill of Ares...
Here my laws shall stand
Unchanged through the hours of the days, the days of
  the years.
And awe, that humbles the heart,
With fear, the brother of awe, from this day
Shall keep the pride of Athenians in check...
I open on this rock
The pure springs of my laws.
Do not taint them
By any expedient shift for advantages.
Protect this court
Which will protect you all
From the headstrong license of any man's will...   19

The verdict for the murderer is tied six to six. To break the tie, the decisive vote is cast by Athena herself, whose wisdom wells up from a source deeper than the intellect. No more, she declares, will the Furies perpetuate the endless spiral of violence. From that day forward, *throughout all time to come,* justice within the Athenian democracy will be rooted in compassion, mercy, and forgiveness.

Only I, Pallas Athene,
Possess the key
That unlocks the thunderbolt of Zeus.
But the time of brute force
Is past.
The day of reasoned persuasion,

57

With its long vision,
With its mercy, its forgiveness,
Has arrived.
The word hurled in anger shall be caught
In a net of gentle words,
Words of quiet strength.   20

Athena then addresses the Furies, admitting that these *appalling creatures* who fully understand the nature of both innocence and guilt are inherently, innately wise. She renames them the *Kindly Ones*, who will return *(k)indness for kindness,* noble women who henceforth will bless Athenian life.

Daughters of timeless darkness,
Enter your subterranean home.
You who know what honour is
And why honour is holy,
Enter the fortress of understanding....
Terrible kindly ones,
Come to your rest
In the flame of torches
And let the voice of every citizen,
With a shout of welcome, be made holy.

Pour out the wine,
Let the pine bough crack and blaze.
Zeus, Father of All,
Guards the city of Athens.
So God and Fate, in a divine marriage,
Are made one in the flesh
Of all our people –
And the voice of their shout is single and holy.   21

In our contemporary system of justice, however, regarding physicians whose innocent error results in either a negligible adjustment for the patient or a medical catastrophe, this culture with its *expedient shift for advantages* and its *headstrong license of any man's will* has tragically, scandalously resurrected the Furies.

There is a movement now for hospitals and doctors to admit to the patient and the family the errors they have innocently committed and apologize for their mistakes, but how *wildly unrealistic* is this expectation of the general public when our collective behavior toward them both has been so abusive for so long! This selfish belief is yet another example of how the public demands that our medical professionals as well as their institutions display not only superhuman ability, but superhuman virtue as well. To be vulnerable is to be in a defenseless position in the presence of an actual threat that could do to one's self and to one's significant others actual harm. In the recent pandemic of opportunistic malpractice lawsuits which prey upon the humanity and vulnerability of the very physicians who are nobly committed to sustaining our lives, we the patients and the patients' families pose a monstrous threat. Health care professionals have learned through decades of hard-won experience that knowledge of their errors can be used for betrayal, public humiliation, losses of millions of dollars, and every conceivable form of public and private pain. It is evidence of their collective wisdom that professionals refuse to disclose their vulnerability except by court order.

To stop this nation's insane pursuit of senseless mercenary litigation, it is **we the laymen** who must pause to consider the colossal repercussions of our initiating unwarranted lawsuits, **we the laymen** who must pause to consider the hundreds of innocent people who will be directly impacted by our selfishness and insatiable greed, **we the laymen** who must actively refuse from a state of shock and disbelief to rush to find a phone. It is **we** who must teach the medical community that we are trustworthy by first demonstrating responsible behavior toward them. Vulnerability between physicians and patients will one day be a mutual validation of our shared humanity, a sanguine confirmation of our shared belief in the fundamental goodness of all, a compassionate ontological acceptance that though our doctors sometimes make unfortunate errors, they have sincerely striven to the maximum of their expertise to *do no harm*. Vulnerability will one day be a shared wisdom and a reciprocal joy, an authenticity which will provide for physicians, patients, and their families that mutual support which selflessly nourishes, respectfully affirms, and lovingly sustains.

CB 80

April 4, 1968

The cast of a single lot restores a house to greatness.

Aeschylus
The Eumenides

STATEMENT BY SENATOR ROBERT F. KENNEDY ON THE

DEATH OF THE REVEREND MARTIN LUTHER KING

RALLY IN INDIANAPOLIS, INDIANA - April 4, 1968

I have bad news for you, for all of our fellow citizens, and people who love peace all over the world, and that is that Martin Luther King was shot and killed tonight.

Martin Luther King dedicated his life to love and to justice for his fellow human beings, and he died because of that effort.

In this difficult day, in this difficult time for the United States, it is perhaps well to ask what kind of a nation we are and what direction we want to move in. For those of you who are black -- considering the evidence there evidently is that there were white people who were responsible -- you can be filled with bitterness, with hatred, and a desire for revenge. We can move in that direction as a country, in great polarization -- black people amongst black, white people amongst white, filled with hatred toward one another.

Or we can make an effort, as Martin Luther King did, to understand and to comprehend, and to replace that violence, that stain of bloodshed that has spread across our land, with an effort to understand with compassion and love.

For those of you who are black and are tempted to be filled with hatred and distrust at the injustice of such an act, against all white people, I can only say that I feel in my own heart the same kind of feeling. I had a member of my family killed, but he was killed by a white man. But we have to make an effort in the United States, we have to make an effort to understand, to go beyond these rather difficult times.

My favorite poet was Aeschylus. He wrote: "In our sleep, pain which cannot forget falls drop by drop upon the heart until, in our own despair, against our will, comes wisdom through the awful grace of God."

What we need in the United States is not division; what we need in the United States is not hatred; what we need in the United States is not violence or lawlessness, but love and wisdom, and compassion toward one another, and a feeling of justice towards those who still suffer within our country, whether they be white or they be black.

So I shall ask you tonight to return home, to say a prayer for the family of Martin Luther King, that's true, but more importantly to say a prayer for our own country, which all of us love -- a prayer for understanding and that compassion of which I spoke.

We can do well in this country. We will have difficult times. We've had difficult times in the past. We will have difficult times in the future. It is not the end of violence; it is not the end of lawlessness; it is not the end of disorder.

But the vast majority of white people and the vast majority of black people in this country want to live together, want to improve the quality of our life, and want justice for all human beings who abide in our land.

Let us dedicate ourselves to what the Greeks wrote so many years ago: to tame the savageness of man and to make gentle the life of this world.

Let us dedicate ourselves to that, and say a prayer for our country and for our people.

During the height of the race riots in 1968, Robert Kennedy stood upon the back of a flatbed truck in the heart of the Indianapolis ghetto and announced to a gathering of African-Americans in the darkness of night that the Rev. Martin Luther King Jr., was dead. No armored car shielded him. No bullet proof vest protected his heart. Defenseless and exquisitely vulnerable, Kennedy announced that King was dead. Amid screams, moans, and muffled cries of anguish, he quoted this immortal passage from *Agamemnon,* the first great tragedy in the trilogy of Aeschylus, *The Oresteia.* His voice calm, his gaze unwavering, he hesitated briefly before the word *despite*...then changed it to *despair.* No one knows if his pause displayed a momentary memory lapse, or if he altered the text to approximate the profound depths of his own private agony, but he quoted as follows –

> *Even in our sleep, pain which cannot forget*
> *Falls drop by drop upon the heart,*
> *Until, in our own despair,*
> *Against our will,*
> *Comes wisdom*
> *Through the awful grace of God.* 23

Though violence continued to blaze all around this country, the city of Indianapolis remained calm. The crowd dispersed into the shadows to grieve and ponder in the privacy of their hearts and homes the overpowering majesty of *the awful grace of God.* Robert Kennedy's cast alone *of a single lot restore(d) a house to greatness.*

America required only one young woman to refuse to move to the back of the bus. India required only one young lawyer to toss a paper into a basket and shake the Western World. It is quite possible that in the reader's own future, an opportunity will arise when you too can bring your gavel down upon the competency of your physician. It is my deepest hope that your impact resounds with compassion, mercy, and forgiveness.

Cʒ ℬↄ

Part II

The Plaintiff's Grasp at Power

*The love of power…at (its) root,
is generally an embodiment of fear.*

Bertrand Russell

Ego States

"Where is your brother Abel?"

"Am I my brother's keeper?"

History's first
crossed transaction.

The psychiatrist, Dr. Eric Berne, created a sensation in the psychological world in 1964 with the publication of his book, *Games People Play*. Though his classic was originally intended for psychological and psychiatric specialists, *Games* skyrocketed overnight to the status of bestseller not only for the professionals but for laymen as well who live, work, and raise families in all walks of life. Berne's fundamental principles strip all human interactions to their most basic, easily understandable essentials, from the most benign *'Good morning'* over coffee to the sophisticated diplomatic repartee preceding, during, and following the massive movements of world wars. No patterns of human speech escaped the astute and sensitive ear of Eric Berne. Games are not contingent upon intellectual acumen, nor are they dependent upon financial status. Beneficial as well as destructive games are played by every human being in every quadrant of this world as well as in every culture, from the most primitive to the most advanced. During the pleasant social situations of picnics and philharmonic concerts as well as in Trauma Centers in the critical urgencies of life and death, the same games are played, because each of us unfortunately is a creature born with a substantial need which from birth to death is constantly frustrated.

When a baby is born, the intense intimacy between that child and its mother is severed forever. From that day forward, the infant, eventually the child, and ultimately the adult seeks to re-establish an equivalent intimacy with his world through the only means which are at the deposal of every conscious human being – social interaction, psychological interplay, and the physical dimension. Realistically, the pace of life affords little time for extended periods of intimacy, and even when quantities of time do present themselves, few adults are sufficiently evolved either emotionally or psychologically to maintain such deep connection with another for any appreciable length. As a result, most adult lives are unfortunately spent trying to satisfy our most essential need through pastimes and through socially acceptable, sometimes socially unacceptable, and sometimes pathetic emotional, psychological, and physical games. In the most drastically reduced, most simplistic form, the adult can satisfy his most elemental need by one of two means – true empathic intimacy which in the contemporary world is a rare treasure, or games which are based upon the interpersonal interplay between the three ego states inherent in everyone.

As a psychiatrist who daily witnessed both functional and dysfunctional behavior, Berne noted that his patients exhibited at certain times conspicuous changes in posture, viewpoint, tone of voice, vocabulary, and various observable behaviors which were accompanied by alterations in feelings. Each set of these characteristics corresponded to a specific change of mind, a specific change in psychic attitude, which would be suddenly displayed in striking contrast to a previously exhibited state. He labeled these coherent systems of feelings and behaviors *ego states*. Berne concluded that each individual is inherently an aggregation of the following states –

1) *The Parent* is an assembly of parental attitudes and behaviors which the client has observed and absorbed from her own assemblage of parental figures. These attitudes may not be truly those of the actual parental figures, but are the child's *perception* of their attitudes.

2) The *Adult* is analogous to one's own internal scientist, one's own internal computer, which impartially investigates and processes objective data. This ego state is essential for the survival of both the individual as well as the human species.

3) The *Child* is the repository of archaic feelings and behaviors, a catalogue of the client's own internal responses to the parental attitudes and behaviors he witnessed during the first few years of life.

Dr. Berne also observed this normal psychological phenomenon, that within both the Parent and Child ego states exist healthy sub-divisions.

1) The Parent includes both the *emotionally nurturing Parent* as well as the *condemning critical Parent*, each state absorbed during the child's early period of growth, each of these two sub-states exhibiting its own unique set of behaviors, body postures, tones of voice, facial expressions, aspects of personality to which upon reflection all readers can resonate.

2) The Child includes both the *spontaneous care-free Child* who happily and creatively smears spaghetti into his hair, as well as the *adapted Child*, who modifies his behavior to the wishes and requirements of his parents as well as to their society by learning to twirl spaghetti at the table with a fork.

In emotionally and psychologically healthy individuals, these three states as well as their subdivisions are carefully segregated from one another, because they are vastly different in how each state perceives its relationships and its world. In the writings of Berne, these states are much more complicated and sophisticated, but for the purposes of this chapter, the individual psyche appears as Parent on top, Adult in the middle, and Child beneath.

Parent nurturing, or critical

Adult data processing

Child carefree, or adapted

Each human interaction, the *transaction,* is thus between two individual sets of these three ego states.

P	emotionally nurturing / critical	P
A	data processing	A
C	playful/adapted	C

When a transaction between people is complementary, the verbal exchange is free from ulterior motives. Playful child can safely interact with emotionally nurturing Parent, and critical Parent can safely disciple a rebellious Child. Gossip can proceed smoothly over coffee between two individuals indulging their mutual critical Parent, and two individuals can exchange needed information without emotional involvement from the data processing computers of their own Adult ego states. As long as the vectors within transactions are straight complementary lines, the communication can proceed indefinitely.

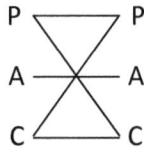

However, various degrees of problems arise when vectors cross. For example, a simple request for information about the most elementary of subjects may sound at first hearing to be an exchange between Adult and Adult, but embedded in the transaction is the uncomfortable feeling that one's self has been somehow shamed by a skillfully concealed critical Parent.

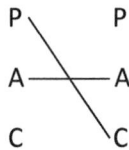

These crossed vectors proliferate in fantastic and extraordinary ways in the exchanges diagramed in Eric Berne's book, dialogues which produce misunderstandings and hard feelings ranging from a simple problem of who after dinner will walk the dog, to who will initiate the first volley of the next world war. It is from these crossed vectors, these embedded ulterior transactions which are always dishonest, manipulative, and intrinsically self-serving, that the games which we play are born.

During an interview, Dr. Berne was somewhat at a loss to explain why games are played to reinforce a specific negative presupposition, where each ulterior and manipulative transaction is designed to ultimately reaffirm a pre-existing belief. The prevalence of the *Now I've Got You* game which is currently played so frequently and with such irrational vehemence by the lay community when initiating unwarranted lawsuits against competent physicians, reinforces society's growing suspicion that all doctors are inadequate, and that few are worthy of trust. Personalized games may reinforce that one's self is filled with guilt, or shame, or powerlessness, or inadequacy for reasons which supposedly are entirely appropriate and correct. These destructive and demoralizing games, composed of a complex series of transactions carefully monitored by one's own Adult ego state, conclude with a confirmation that one's perceptual matrix is a reliable constant. In a world of ever-changing phenomena, games conclude with the assurance that despite the vicissitudes and fluctuations of existence, the predictable negative reinforcement of one's preferred games necessarily means that one's very self is stable. This may be the reason why manipulative and dishonest games are played with such persistence within this country which is presumed to be so self-aware.

Those individuals who are labeled more mature are those who approach life largely from their Adult, with their spontaneous Child, adapted Child, and the varied displays of nurturing or critical Parent peeking out only occasionally. This highly intellectual approach to the circumstances of life through the Adult ego state is detrimental in the world of the arts where the creative energies of the spontaneous Child must necessarily be encouraged to freely flourish. However, during the drama of a medical crisis, it is one's ability to coolly process incoming data through one's Adult which will prove most valuable.

All patients, families, as well as their medical professionals are highly skilled in the games which serve their unarticulated needs most effectively, because we practice them to perfection even on the most uneventful of days. It is therefore understandable that during the heightened emotions of a medical crisis which may include physician error, when laymen with their favorite games collide with medical personnel who indulge as well in their own, little provocation is needed for those same games to intensify into exaggerated and ruthless forms, exploding almost instantly into a lawsuit for medical malpractice in the behavior of patients or loved ones whose critical powers of coherent thought originating in their Adult ego state have been temporarily overridden by the primitive reflexes of fight, flight, or freeze. It is also necessary to realize that in the Emergency Room setting, the doctor himself as well as the hospital staff are sunk in their own varying depths of fight, flight, or freeze, not only because of possible error, but also because of decades of aggressively hostile behaviors, lodged in their collective memory, which have been leveled at them by the general public who have childishly and sometimes hatefully abused the medical profession for so long. This heightened emotional interplay between family and hospital staff is the perfect environment for the game of *Lottery Lawsuit* to foment.

Every moment of every day in the lives of every person contains the latent potential of trauma. In preparation for this atomic collision of family and professionals within this explosive Emergency Room environment of distrust and shock, it will hopefully serve a productive purpose for the reader to study in advance the three games which could very well be instinctively played by the patient, spouse, and family as well as by the medical professionals themselves during a crisis of life and death, which may unfortunately include the stressor of medical miscalculation. A mercenary lawsuit is fundamentally a desperate grasp at power originating within the scared and disoriented Child ego state of the potential plaintiff. By examining the instant when these three

71

common games converge, such a lawsuit which stems from primal fear can hopefully be avoided.

Medical malpractice suits are now pandemic. Their sheer number indicate that the general public now considers it a rite of passage into some deviant form of adulthood to announce with perverted pride, '*I sued my doctor*,' and not only receive a potentially handsome financial settlement, but also receive abundant praise from this society which now considers the pursuit of *Lottery Lawsuit* a responsible and respectable form of adult activity. Since the dynamics of societal games are passed down from generation to generation, the very concept of raising children meaning to teach the receptive child what games to appropriately play, it is tragic that children now are learning from this nationwide insanity that they themselves will necessarily be required to play this same game of persecuting their medical professionals when the children themselves become adults. Equally tragic is that while experiencing the agony of their parents embroiled in the uproar of litigation, children of physicians and nurses themselves learn never to pursue a career in medicine. It is hoped that readers of this book will become aware of the strong tendency within their own natures to revert in a medical crisis to the specific games with which they are undoubtedly most familiar, and are consequently prepared to enter a trauma situation without the dishonesty, manipulation, and selfishness inherent in games, but rather with a depth of sincerity, selflessness, rational focus, and emotional equanimity after driving white-knuckled behind an EMT truck, or after receiving that dreaded phone call from the hospital in the middle of the night.

CR ED

Games

*What sort of space is that which separates a man
from his fellows and makes him solitary?
I have found that no exertion of the legs can bring two minds
much nearer to one another.*

Henry D. Thoreau
Walden

The games which all people play are conceived within the total receptivity, innocence, and bliss of childhood, when one's whole life spreads before one filled with nothing but fantasized happiness and good fortune, where never a cloud will darken one's landscape, where no violent storms will interrupt one's peace, and no tears or heartbreak will dare to impair one's joy. It is a time of fairy tales and absolute certainty, where every little girl is a princess and every princess marries her prince, and all are destined to live happily ever after in a castle in the clouds.

The poet, Dylan Thomas, has artistically rendered this fairy-tale era not only with stunning imagery, but also with pin-point emotional accuracy in his masterpiece *Fern Hill*. This poem expresses the years when the poet himself, as a child who spent summers on his aunt's dairy farm in Wales, *was young and easy under the apple boughs...happy as the grass was green...*when *Under the new made clouds and happy as the heart was long...*the young Dylan *ran (his) heedless ways.* Within irrepressibly lilting Gaelic meter, the poet articulates the dumb-founded delight and astonished admiration of the very young whose energies are suddenly unleashed into the exuberance of Nature, when all of life is, as it were, the very first days of creation, when *The sky gathered again / And the sun grew round that very day.* The predominant color of this poem of joy is appropriately the green of hope, the sustaining color of life. To the fledging eyes of Dylan Thomas, even *fire* is *green as grass,* and children are *green and golden,* fresh in their *morning songs.* For five of the poem's six stanzas, the young poet is immersed in the splendors of Eden with both childish purity and exquisite naiveté, abiding in the sheer rapture of youth embracing the first five days of creation. 24

But in the sixth stanza, reminiscent of the sixth day of creation and the advent of Man, the imagery darkens, the *shadow* appears as well as the confinement of the *swallow thronged loft,* when *the moon...is always rising* because it is always dusk. No longer blissfully unaware *under the apple boughs,* a child running his *heedless ways,* the adult poet is fully aware that once and for all the forbidden mythological fruit has been consumed. Man's consciousness of time has been born as he, aware now of himself as a conscious, living creature who at one time came to be, must one day inevitably die. The adult poet realizes only upon mature reflection that in his era of unknowing innocence, *Time* nevertheless had *held (him) green and dying / Though (he) sang in (his) chains like the sea.*   25

The fairy-tale existence of the poet's early life is shattered by the evolving consciousness of adulthood and those painful experiences which prompt moral maturation and spiritual growth. Not even the poet's fairy tale of his own artistic making is destined to last perpetually. No one lives happily ever after. There is no ideal relationship, no ideal marriage, no ideal birth, and certainly no ideal death. No one, however fortunate in this world, lives a mortal existence free from the agony of pain, disappointment, and various intensities of heartbreak. The poet perfectly expresses that pivotal moment when the illusion of bliss shatters into the stark reality of every human life; time, death, and the potentially tragic are our ever-present companions.

The fairy tales of Europe, upon which American fairy tales are based, are gruesome, shocking, brutal, and often disgusting stories of nightmare imagery rather than images exploited within romanticized Hollywood film. The connotation of the ideal has been forfeited in Disney's European counterpart to display the often sinister subconscious forces which motivate our darkest desires. The first selection of tales, though designated for children, was regarded as unsuitable for the young. It is a moment of historical serendipity that the first edition was published as *'Grimm.'* But the idealized Western fairy tales, which are methodically ingrained into the conscious minds of nearly every American child from infancy on up, portray images of that same utter perfection which dominates the first five stanzas of *Fern Hill.* This idyllic expectation of eternal bliss coupled with our national pioneer mythology that every American is inherently master of his existence and captain of his ship, has indelibly imprinted the minds of generations with the certainty that they themselves can dictate their life and dominate their individual fate. Though this unrealistic expectation may be a fortuitous energy source for the dogged acquiring of one's education and the firm establishing of one's career, this often unshakable belief may unfortunately lead them as adults to the mythological unreality of the *Just World Hypothesis.*

Just World proponents believe that it is their own actions and inherent inclinations which cause life to bestow upon them consequences which their personal preferences define as good, will reward each individual and by extension, one's family or social group with all that is beneficial and, according to each individual's perceptions, with all that is personally assessed as wholesome. The Just World creedal belief is predictable, consequential, and supposedly morally appropriate. It is analogous to the primitive scientific assumption that since the universe revolves around the earth, all is right with the world. This simplistic view is inextricably interwoven with the individual's support of the very principle upon which this belief system is grounded: the selfish, the self-centered, and the largely unconscious drive to simply seek pleasure at every opportunity and to avoid pain at all costs.

Human life all round this globe provides ample evidence which disproves this hypothesis each and every day and in nearly every circumstance. Consequently, Just World proponents have devised ingenious strategies which are sometimes rational and sometimes uniquely irrational to maintain their foundational principle that actions have predictable and appropriate consequences, while explaining away all that is *unjust* by denigrating those who suffer as being inherently inferior to them. A well-known American belief is that those who are poor deserve poverty because they are supposedly morally or racially inferior, in contrast to those who acquire wealth because they supposedly deserve it. Another example is that when an individual, family, or social group suffers tragedy, their pain is inflicted by the universe supposedly because they themselves invited it. This hypothesis is a simplistic cognitive bias that human existence is morally fair, spiritually equitable, that one's most noble efforts will be rewarded, and that those who deviate from one's own ideal will be punished. Such beliefs are ultimately delusional, but are nevertheless upheld by millions who unfortunately may appear in the doctor's Trauma Center following innocent medical error. To restore the proponent's equilibrium in the face of a disaster which to her *should not have happened* because the patient *did not deserve it*, the potential plaintiff, desperate to return to the perceived righteousness of a Just World, has no choice but to denigrate the competency of the physician as well as the integrity of his hospital by grasping at power by filing a vengeful lawsuit.

Added to the frustrated millions who daily attempt to believe in a Just World are the millions who believe in the obscenity called *Prosperity Theology*, which is based upon a perverse mauling of the teachings of Christ, that those who *"lay up for (themselves) treasures on earth where moth and rust (supposedly) do not corrupt"* are fulfilling the highest ideals of a morally unrecognizable interpretation of the Gospels. Despite Christ's assertion to the contrary, that a rich man has no more ability to *"pass through the eye of a needle"* than, for that matter, does *"a camel,"* prosperity proponents believe that financial success is the will of God, that the more one gives to prosperity churches and individual figureheads of the prosperity movement, the more wealth will be showered upon one as a spiritual reward. The most innocent verses from both the Hebrew and Greek scriptures are twisted to support this secular perversion. Prosperity Theology is popular within poor populations of the United States, among underprivileged whites and blacks, Hispanics, and immigrants, but is embraced as well by America's middle class who crave more and more wealth and possessions to satisfy their insatiable greed. Proponents of this theology as well as proponents of the Just World may appear as parents, loved ones, spouses, or adult children of the patient in the Emergency Room following medical error. In addition to both these groups will inevitably appear those who will be tempted to pursue a mercenary lawsuit because of *opportunism.*   26

In its most positive definition, opportunism is the ability of an organism to take advantage of its circumstances to foster the survival of itself or its group.   This life-sustaining skill, inherent in our very emotional and psychological makeup, is the underlying principle of physical evolution. Opportunistic tendencies are known to all, to every member of all walks of life, in every stratum of wealth or poverty, as well as in every stratum of intellectual development. Opportunism cuts through class distinction, nationality, race, religion, and creed. It is a survival skill which has served the purposes of Mother Nature for millennia. This principle so grand and of such cosmic proportions is also daily lived in countless homes across the United States, as the frustrated parent takes advantage of a momentary diversion to place a spoon of mashed carrot in an astonished toddler's mouth.

But like every other quality inherent in human nature, opportunism has a dark and sinister underside, as the ability to foster life can be consciously used against it for destruction. The pejorative definition of opportunism is the taking advantage of life's circumstances for selfish advantage with little or no regard for the welfare of others, by forfeiting, discarding as situationally irrelevant, or by temporarily surrendering one's own moral principles which, before the circumstance arose, were held in high regard. It capitalizes upon the weakness and *hamartia* of another, using his errors as advantageous for one's personal advancement. Opportunism considers how the greatest gain can be afforded one's self, family, or group at the least personal cost, and often responds to group, societal, or legal pressure to abandon one's moral matrix in the pursuit of wealth, notoriety, and influence. Opportunism inherently implies the moral dilemma of pitting the selfish interests of one against the best interests of many, a moral crisis which is easily solved by either jettisoning the principles which one formerly held dear, or reinforcing by example that those ethics indeed had *never* been the guiding principles of one's life. When all moral principles are temporarily or permanently abandoned, and the greater good is viewed as an obstacle to one's own drives, it becomes a matter of expedience to sacrifice one's integrity as having no value at all in contrast to what can possibly be gained. A statistic which should humiliate every American is that the higher the potential for gain at the least possible cost, the more likely will personal integrity be forfeited.

In terms of physician error which unintentionally harms a patient, the way of the potential plaintiff who has abandoned her moral matrix is then opened wide to pursue the mercenary, to disrupt the lives and livelihoods of so many, to propel a lawsuit, even unto the possible suicide of the doctor, with the hope of emptying the deepest pockets not only of the physician but of his hospital too, while slyly cloaking her opportunism within the fraudulent belief that she has a noble obligation not only to her fellow human beings, but to the other patients of the doctor as well. By forfeiting personal dignity and with a woeful lack of self-awareness, plaintiffs of illegitimate lawsuits, for personal gain, actively strive to inflict upon the doctor and his profession deliberate harm. Members of these groups, as well as others, present in the Trauma Center as loved ones of the patient, each possessing pre-established biases, irrational fairy-tale dreams, as well as an inherent ability, which seems to be encoded into our very DNA, to take full advantage of the misfortune of others to satisfy personal greed. Some are destined to suddenly encounter full force the devastating consequences of physician error, then play with the doctor and hospital staff three significant and universally known games.

If It Weren't For You

Berne presents *If It Weren't For You* as one of the most common games played by married couples. Though the dynamics of this game may be fiercely intense during the early years of their relationship, older seasoned members of the marital state may indulge in this game with a good deal of humor as a celebration that, as a result of their decades of sincerely working on their relationship, they now have the enjoyment of playing this game with self-awareness and a sense of fun.   Miss A, whose regressed nature doubts her ability to maintain her Adult ego state in the outside world, marries Mr. A because he, a domineering man, will shelter and protect her from interacting with the outside world.   Though the psychic requirements of the now Mrs. A are fulfilled by her repressive marriage, she nevertheless frequently expresses in frustration, *'If it weren't for you, I'd be having fun out in the world.'* Mr. A, who likewise has a submerged horror of abandonment, replies with some cloaked variation of *'Don't you dare, because I'm afraid of desertion.'* Since both husband and wife are rooted in antiquated fears buried in their Child ego states, both their needs for mutual protection and assurance are satisfied by the underlying dynamics of this game…until that momentous day when Mr. A, fed up with Mrs. A's frequent complaining, gives her permission to pursue her life in the world.   Mrs. A, who quickly discovers that her unconscious fears are indeed realities, that she truly does have difficulty maintaining her Adult in social contexts, quickly returns home to the former dynamic which has supported the couple's mutual needs since they wed. This game would cease if both Mr. and Mrs. A mutually acknowledged through their Adult the fears of their Child ego states, thus deepening their relationship into a new dimension, but because of the couple's fear of intimacy, the game remains a permanent fixture throughout their marriage. The dynamics of *If It Weren't For You* are considerably more complex and sophisticated in Berne's book, but for the purposes of its application to medical malpractice lawsuits, it is obvious how the superficial aspects of this game can be instinctively transplanted to the Emergency Room.

Regardless of his personality, character, or how sincerely he presents himself, every ER doctor wearing a white coat represents the domineering husband. He necessarily has power not only over the patient, but over the spouse and family as well.   In this high-stress situation of trauma, where stranger encounters stranger in an alien environment of machines and tubes, mutual suspicion and fear, it is quite natural for the loved one to react to such perceived authority from the ego state of her rebellious Child. This unfortunate response can lead to dramatic exchanges with the ER staff, and may accelerate and intensify the behavior of the loved one into the need for physical restraints to control the potential plaintiff. The game *If it Weren't For You* may begin even before the discovery of physician error, since the loved one, whose rebellion and panic make her unaware of how she is prompting this emotional crisis, holds the doctor and his staff responsible for humiliating her by treating her like an unruly little girl. After the mistake is discovered, however, the game intensifies, fueled by the energy inherent in horror, as the error itself levels a frontal assault upon all the fundamentals which had previously served as the supportive structures of the potential plaintiff's very life.

'If it weren't for you, this medical disaster would never have happened. If it weren't for you and this hospital, no one would have been harmed. If it weren't for you, I could continue to believe that the progression of my life was under my control, and that I and those I love would receive only what we want, because that is what we deserve. If it weren't for you and your staff, God would still be living in my personal heaven, doing as I personally please by providing only what I want, and I could persist in living within the illusion of my fairy tale.'

In his poem *We Have the Fairy Tales by Heart*, Dylan Thomas describes this awful moment of cosmic revelation when the dearest myths of childhood are destroyed. Previously the youth of *Fern Hill* was protected by the illusions embedded in fairy tales, and as a result was no longer threatened by *the thunder's first note,* was no longer fearful of God as *the walker in the garden.* But when the potential plaintiff, who like the poet was formerly protected by her own assemblage of fairy tales, discovers the dire consequences of physician error, the poet assures us that all *the fibs for children* as well as all *the old spells are undone.* The loved one feels the terror that *the walker in the garden* has mocked her childish world order, shattered her untested composure, imposed a psychic chaos onto her false existence, destroyed her every superficial grounding, and suspended her and her family over an infinite Abyss of the cosmic unknown. The terrified potential plaintiff will no doubt translate her disorientation as a deliberately inflicted humiliation from the dictatorial doctor within her wounded and horrified Child ego state. But rather than sincerely feel this agony to her very depths and allow it to expand her spiritual horizons into previously unknown dimensions, she instead lashes out in a desperate grasp for power from her self-righteous critical Parent in a threatened pursuit of a vengeful, mercenary lawsuit.   27

See What You Made Me Do

At this point begins the game *See What You Made Me Do*, another marital game which Berne describes as *a three star marriage buster*. Mr. B, who is totally absorbed in an occupation, who is unsociable for the moment, is interrupted by Mrs. B or a member of their family. In irritation, he responds to the intruder by displaying a minor *accident*, and through varying intensities of annoyance exclaims, *'See what you made me do.'* This game would not exist within the B family, if Mr. B simply expressed through his Adult his need to be uninterrupted for specific lengths of time for his personal pursuit, and in response his family sincerely and respectfully responded through their individual Adult ego states to his articulated need. But without risking that moment of family intimacy, Mrs. B and their children learn over the years to leave Mr. B alone when he is so occupied.

This game easily transplants to the Trauma Center, as the family wishes to preserve their previously held beliefs about doctors, life, God, the Just World, and their own immunity against suffering and death, because that is what they deserve. Berne explains that the precipitating event which initiates this game is the threat of emotional intimacy, which in the case of medical error, is the exposure of the family to the broader dimensions of the spiritual life. But the horrified loved one, as a *flight* reaction away from the holy which translates into a *fight* reaction toward the physician responsible for the error, searches for the nearest phone while threatening –

'I have no choice, Doctor. See what you make me do. I must file a lawsuit. If it weren't for you, this would never have happened. I have no choice now but to find a phone. See what you make me do.'

Though up to now, these two games have been presented as played solely by the patient and family, it is essential that the professionals become aware that they themselves foster the atmosphere where these dynamics flourish by playing these same two games with families, but from the opposite perspective.   All medical professionals enter their careers with idealism and joy, fully expecting that in a Just World, their sincere efforts to display toward their patients competence and compassion will be rewarded by reciprocal displays of gratitude and respect.   Though it is admittedly an occupational hazard to receive various degrees of abusive behavior while caring for those in the throes of excruciating pain, depths of shock, as well as drug addiction, nurses in Emergency Rooms frequently complain that they are routinely bit, slapped, scratched, verbally denigrated, and spit upon by those who are entirely mentis and self-aware.   One ER doctor wears leather gloves, so he can drive home without teeth marks in his hands. These patients lash out in an opportunistic fury at those committed to inflict upon them no harm, unburdening themselves of some degree of their primal rage by leveling at hospital personnel the game *Now I've Got You, You Son of a Bitch*. Unfortunately, this creates an internal monologue in the caregiver which by now sounds familiar.

'If it weren't for you, I'd still be happy in my profession. If it weren't for you, I'd still have my ideals. I'd look forward to coming to work, because my heart would still be open. If it weren't for you, I wouldn't now be self-protective and shut down, but because of you, I'm seriously doubting my ability and my willingness to remain in this profession.'

Now the staff of the Trauma Center, like the focused Mr. B, plays *See What You Made Me Do* with the potential plaintiff. They abandon her and her family to cope with their tragedy as best they can. Health care providers have learned through years, even decades of hard-won experience that families in crisis are volatile, that they exhibit their fight reflex by displaying snap judgments, jumping to irrational conclusions, processing information inadequately, and exhibiting poor listening skills. Their emotions are on the surface; they wear their hearts on their sleeve. Sunk as well in the primal fear of their Child ego state, potential plaintiffs tend to translate every action and every word spoken by the ER staff as a deliberate slap against the family.

Up to now though, there has been no action taken by the potential plaintiff toward the medical establishment except a flurry of verbal accusations plus displays of various degrees of hostility and rage, which are inherent characteristics of the first two games. Then a merciful moment materializes. Between the accusations of *If It Weren't For You,* the withdrawal of the staff in *Look What You Made Me Do,* and the deliberate legal action of *Now I've Got You*, a brief hiatus appears, an interval during which the potential plaintiff, who is filled with terror and disillusionment within her disoriented Child ego state, who longs to grasp at power to stabilize her inner world, could potentially be talked down from her psychic ledge altogether by the hospital staff itself before she attempts to pursue a vengeful lawsuit. This interval may be exceedingly brief, so the procedure to de-escalate the potential plaintiff with emotional and psychological sensitivity would need to be a predetermined hospital policy known by all employees. But if that interim is not appreciated by the hospital staff as mercifully opportunistic for the doctor's career as well as for the hospital's very survival, the potential plaintiff will become an *actual* plaintiff who grabs the nearest phone and contacts her attorney. Even before the medical records are finalized, she may call her lawyer.

Once that attorney's authoritative voice is heard, and the words are spoken, *'It's good you contacted me this early. We'll obtain those records, and get this suit going,'* the plaintiff's shaken interior world begins to stabilize. Backed by the power of her attorney speaking to her as the innocent victim from his nurturing Parent ego state, and speaking against the doctor from his condemning Parent ego state, her previously held beliefs begin the process of shifting back into place, her

Just World suddenly comes back into view, her humiliation is ended because her power has been reintroduced, and her childish belief in her immunity against suffering and death is re-established, because this medical error, according to the myopic perspective of herself and her attorney, was truly undeserved. If the hiatus between these first two games and the third is not grasped by the medical community as mercifully opportunistic both for the career of the unfortunate physician as well as for the financial stability of his hospital, the third game played by the plaintiff and her attorney will begin - *Now We've Got Them, Those Sons of Bitches.* This legal retaliation will be aimed at both the doctor and his hospital, a destructive game which will soon explode into the massive proportions of a vengeful and mercenary lawsuit for medical malpractice.

The seeds of this particular form of *Lottery Lawsuit* could be initially sown during the introductory interaction of the potential plaintiff with the medical professionals when she and her family first entered the hospital or Trauma Center, seeds which could very well be encouraged to sprout during the family's stay at that hospital, as well as to grow to maturity during the coming weeks. Such opportunities presented themselves to me during my husband's final crisis and during the weeks subsequent to his death. It is this unfortunate dynamic which will now be addressed.

ॐ ৪০

Entrance, Duration, Aftermath

...in peace permit
Our just and lineal entrance...

William Shakespeare
King John

There is further compliment of leave-taking...

William Shakespeare
King Lear

Just as it is imperative that the potential plaintiff not contact an attorney while in a state of shock, it is equally important that hospitals examine their policies of how they interact with the family during the medical emergency as well as during the week immediately following the crisis. These are the situational stress points for the loved ones which could easily prompt the desire to seek revenge against doctors, hospitals, and against the medical profession as a whole by initiating a mercenary lawsuit.

When my husband was first diagnosed nearly twelve years ago, one of his physicians assured him that he could very well live to old age and die from the flu. To that unrealistic expectation, my husband clung with all his strength for the next decade. As a result of his unfailing hope and the force of his denial, three doctors were unwilling to tell him or me the truth about how his disease was mercilessly advancing, or about the myriad complications which would almost certainly present as his disease relentlessly progressed. By the time he was clearly in the end-stage of every complication, no doctor was willing to give him a life expectancy. As a result, we were never eligible for any of the services provided by Hospice, neither were we eligible for any home health care. The entire burden of his disease and its complications fell upon me. Throughout his last year, I could clearly see that he was dying, but nearly every person in our family responded in support of my husband's denial. If it had not been for the common sense of my oldest daughter, I would have been utterly alone.

During his last extended hospitalization, I desperately sought information from one of his primary doctors by literally blocking his way out of the hospital room. Glaring at him, I demanded, *"Talk to me!"* He said one sentence which truly horrified me – the only straight answer I had heard from him since my husband began as his patient five years before. Pleading for information, I asked our chiropractor whose father died from the same disease. He said that judging from the symptoms I described, my husband had only about eighteen more months to live, a prediction which unfortunately proved true very nearly to the day. However, because he was a chiropractor and not a medical doctor, his prediction held no weight with Hospice.

I endured ten years of half-truths and polite deceptions, not realizing at the time that the profound reticence of those physicians to discuss with me any facts with any degree of sincerity was because an imaginary judge, jury, malpractice attorneys, as well as newscasters and newspaper reporters were listening to our every conversation. The threat of an imagined lawsuit suppressed all honest dialogue. Though their reticence apparently was beneficial and self-protective for them, it provided no protection for me. The work load, financial burden, and emotional strain of my husband's last five years caused my oldest daughter to worry constantly that I would die from exhaustion before her father. During his last week, his doctors seemed to withdraw their interest, as though they knew he was about to die. It was from this state of emotional and physical exhaustion, as well as from a decade of being politely and professionally ignored, that I arrived at the morning of my husband's final crisis. By the time I arrived at the Trauma Center doors, I was already poised for a lawsuit.

Very early one dark winter morning, I found my husband lying on the tile floor in the utility room in front of the washer with his head wedged in a bucket. Because the paramedics would not allow me to ride in the truck with them, I proceeded alone to the hospital, driving at only twenty miles an hour on icy country roads, with snow blowing so fiercely across open fields that I had to watch the side of the road, because the center line was invisible. Though it undoubtedly took only minutes for the EMT truck to transport him to the nearby hospital, it took me nearly twenty-five, because driving conditions were so treacherous. Near the hospital, I made a wrong turn and found myself in a neighborhood I did not recognize. A pickup truck was approaching about three blocks away. To catch the attention of that driver so that hopefully he would stop, I turned on my flashers, blinked my headlights, rolled down my window, and began to make wide and frantic gestures. When the truck showed no sign of slowing down, I swerved into his lane in utter desperation, risking a head-on collision. Mercifully for us both, the driver stopped and gave me directions. Minutes later, I arrived at the hospital. In sheer panic that my husband was already dead or would die before I could see him, I consciously disregarded hospital policy that I was to park in the visitors' lot. Instead I rammed my car into a snowbank in the ambulance bay, and hurrying to the trauma entrance, banged with both fists on the doors which in my heightened emotional state appeared to soar upward at least thirty feet. Two minutes later, I was expected to dialogue with that attending physician from my unemotional, dispassionate Adult ego state.

Though our brief exchange could be viewed by some as humorous, our dialogue was for me a supremely challenging intellectual effort. Not only was I on the verge of total emotional and physical collapse, but my heart was hammering in my chest with such intensity that individual heartbeats disappeared entirely into one solid wall of stress. During our conversation, every transaction was crossed. No vectors were complementary straight lines. Though his questions sounded as though they originated from his Adult, my own Adult ego state intuited that he was assessing me from his critical Parent to my Child. By observing my ability to maintain eye contact, by listening to the tone of my voice, as well as observing other non-verbals, he correctly anticipated that I would be able to bear the horror behind the curtain without lashing out at him or his staff.

During this supreme crisis point of my life, my Adult likewise had to correctly evaluate him as though I were the critical Parent and he the Child. It was only because of my knowledge of psychology and the interplay of games that I could correctly assess that physician. By observing his own non-verbals, and by listening to the various strengths of his affirmations to my statements, I correctly deduced that my husband now suffered from two new medical conditions of which I was previously unaware, that because of the doctor's obvious fear, something must be terribly wrong, and that within hours, if not within minutes, I would be a widow. Our mutual search for insight into the other's character yielded accurate results, but by means based upon crossed transactions and subtle manipulations which were slightly humiliating for me. Our conversation established in me so little trust that I wondered if he truly were my husband's physician. I concluded that the doctors responsible for the resuscitation must have left. Unfortunately, but accurately, I came to the conclusion that I was in an environment of mutual distrust and suspicion, that for my own safety as well as to accomplish my supreme desire to remain always with my husband, I should be cautious when dealing with that hospital's personnel. The isolation inherent in *See What You Made Me Do* was now mutual. It was established as the definitive dynamic for us both.

My oldest daughter drove a greater distance over narrow country roads in blinding gusts of snow, and was greeted at the visitors' entrance by a nurse with whom she had an almost identical conversation. The nurse was stern, and cleverly manipulated from my daughter as well the information the hospital required. Independent of me, my daughter arrived at the same conclusions as I did. Two family members, at two different entrances, interacting with two different genders in two different areas of expertise, we arrived at the same conclusion – emotionally and psychologically, she and I as the loved ones of the patient were on our own. Only minutes after our arrival, we both felt the distrust and condescension of the staff. We both intuited that we somehow were viewed as the potential enemy. The hospital's fear of our family as well as its emotional aloofness from us were palpable. Even before the medical records were finalized, even before my husband's various physicians had been notified that he was near death, even before I was allowed in to see him, and even before I realized that a miscalculation had occurred, the seeds of a vengeful lawsuit had been sown.

During the last sixty hours of my husband's life, few members of the hospital staff risked eye contact with me, and all but two were emotionally distant. No chaplain or social worker was sent to us. No emotional or psychological support was offered. Because I was totally riveted upon my husband, our children who were suffering various depths of denial and shock were left alone to cope with their ordeal as best they could. I learned later that even the chaplain himself supported avoidance of eye contact with families who could potentially sue. Even our friends who briefly visited were in shock. If it had not been for two ICU nurses who related to me with understanding, I would have endured the ordeal of those sixty hours largely alone, bearing my tragedy with my own internal strength because no exterior strength from the hospital was offered.

It was inevitable that I would encounter nurses who were burnt out, who made comments in my husband's presence which were clearly inappropriate, hopefully not because those nurses were inherently indifferent, but because they apparently viewed detachment as a necessary evil to maintain their personal sanity. During their comments I leaned into my husband's ear so that he would hear my voice and not theirs. The comment of one nurse was so *wildly* inappropriate that in any other social context, I would have aggressively retaliated. As it was, I simply stared that individual down. The combination of casual conversation in the presence of a man who was obviously nothing more than a viable corpse, my own emotional isolation as well as the agony of his approaching death, could have easily provided even more support for a retaliatory lawsuit, because the hospital itself was nurturing the climate in which hostility could thrive.

The silence of that hospital was also conspicuous during the week after my husband's funeral. His first extended hospitalization took place at that same institution where five years later, he would sadly die. After that first crisis, I received a phone call which inquired how my husband and I were coping with the increasing severity of his disease. Later that week, I also received a questionnaire upon which we rated the services the hospital had provided. Our mutual response was highly positive, because the on-call doctors, the staff of nurses, as well as the friendly and compassionate voice who phoned had treated us as though we were valued friends.

How strikingly different was our family's experience at that same hospital during my husband's final crisis, when apparently the threat of a lawsuit dominated the minds of the staff. Though I was surprised at the emotional distance at the institution where before we had felt such support, I was even more surprised that during the week following his death, no one from that hospital called to offer condolences or to inquire how I was managing my loss. It was not only the absence of emotional support during the final crisis which could have triggered a lawsuit, using the physician's miscalculation as the legal cause, but also the absence of support following my husband's death which could easily prompt some families to reinforce their pre-established beliefs that all hospitals are uncaring and only interested in their own protection. They may think it entirely appropriate to acquiesce to societal pressure, that indeed it is a responsible and necessary act not only for one's family but for the general public as well to initiate an opportunistic lawsuit to prove a vengeful point. Game had prompted game had prompted game had prompted game until *Lottery Lawsuit* was the next inevitable step in a self-destructive progression.

CB EO

Institutional Complicity

What lies behind us
And what lies before us
Are tiny matters
Compared to what lies within us.

Anonymous

95

Hospitals unknowingly encourage the initiation of *Lottery Lawsuit* by playing the same games with families that families play with them. Every *If It Weren't For You* is countered by the same dynamic, and every *See What You Made Me Do* is met by the same game. However, this institutional complicity runs far deeper than superficial games, because a medical crisis for which the family was not adequately prepared can leave imprinted upon the mind a memory which is not only a permanent scar, but can be an open psychic wound which unfortunately can result in varying degrees of disability.

Every vengeful lawsuit for medical malpractice originates within the angry Child ego state, but anger is never a primary emotion, no matter how much the *fight* reflex is stressed. Anger is a *concealing* emotion which cloaks the more intense emotion hiding beneath. Anger is often a cover for the pain of humiliation or sudden shame, a cloak for the agony of abandonment or the terror of threatened loss. Depending upon the psychic state of the individual as well as her prior history, innumerable emotions may serve as prompts which require the strength of anger or the power of rage as a merciful defense against the primary emotion which in the moment is too painful for that individual to bear.

I felt a flash of anger when the doctor pulled back the ER curtain and revealed my husband's face so utterly disfigured. My anger not only cloaked my agonized compassion for the man whom I had loved for half a century, it also cloaked the pain of my personal humiliation. Even before I ran to my husband, I realized that because I had not been prepared for his ghastly appearance, I had been set up to fail – to respond with emotional hysteria, or to require physical restraints for abusive behavior, or to simply faint dead away in an act of ultimate psychic withdrawal. In one way or another, the staff apparently assumed that I would fall beneath their standard of acceptable behavior, and therefore judge me negatively if I could not perform in this supreme crisis with supreme emotional equanimity. It was solely because of the negative assessment my daughter and I had made when we first entered that Trauma Center that I was able to see this set-up as an unconscious variation of *Now We've Got You, You Son of a Bitch*.

The existential payoff of that game would have been in favor of hospital personnel – that they can bear up emotionally because they are innately superior, and families who cannot bear up under staged and premeditated shock are innately inferior to them. I refused to play a variation of *Now We've Got You*. I refused to satisfy anyone's projections that I was an aging child. After my initial scream into my husband's ear, I remained emotionally controlled until after his funeral. I consciously reclaimed my self-respect, both as a self-affirming measure, and also as an act of deliberate two-year-old defiance against adults who held me responsible for superhuman emotional control under superhuman emotional duress. My intuition I had sensed when I first arrived at that hospital was confirmed at that curtain - that our family was in an environment of games and manipulation, and we should exercise caution. Another support for a vengeful lawsuit against the medical profession as a whole had been provided.

While writing Part One of this book, I wondered how families could maintain enough rage toward their physician to sustain a permanent negative stance against him throughout the years necessary to resolve a medical malpractice lawsuit. I imagine now that their fuel is most likely generated from chronic PTSD.

Post-Traumatic Stress Disorder affects millions today in the United States and around the world. Though this syndrome is most often associated with veterans who have either witnessed or personally suffered from the horrors of war, hundreds of thousands of civilians suffer the same symptoms as veterans, because they have survived such a common occurrence as a car crash. PTSD is a serious anxiety disorder which arises after witnessing, from a state of helplessness, the sudden threat of possible death to one's self or another, or the sudden loss of personal integrity to one's self or another, especially one whom one loves. The experience of the trauma is so seared upon the mind by the tsunami of defensive chemicals which at that time poured into the bloodstream, that consciousness is permanently altered. At the moment of psychic impact, the brain is literally rewired. The trauma then becomes an event from which there is no escape, because it seems to be happening over and over in an eternal present, an eternal now, a life-altering event of such significance that it stubbornly refuses to slip from the present tense into one's historic past.

Those who suffer from this syndrome, whether soldiers or civilians, report the same symptoms. During the day, they experience recurrent flashbacks of the event, intrusive thoughts and feelings over which they have no control. Nights are disturbed by nightmares which eventually cause the sufferer to fear sleep itself. They will be hyper-vigilant, hyper-aroused, constantly on the lookout for the slightest hint of danger, hearing and perceiving every minor incident as though each is life-threatening. Since most of the mind is preoccupied with the trauma as the mind simultaneously attempts to protect the victim from further harm, concentration skills are seriously reduced, because the ever-present threat of extinction occupies all one's energies. Many other symptoms qualify as classic manifestations of this terrible psychic burden, which usually begins shortly after the trauma and can last for several weeks, months, or in some cases for years. Tragically, the merciless, unforgiving nature of PTSD drives some to embrace suicide as the only means of certain relief. Though PTSD is the result of a catastrophic infusion of unbearable psychic pain, it fundamentally results from the passive superimposition upon the mind of one or more traumatic images.

Visual images throughout history have been a powerful means to elicit from the viewer some depth of emotional response. Great artists often include significant ambiguities in their works to force viewers to identify more profoundly with the painting, because viewers themselves must necessarily project onto the canvas the details which the artist deliberately omitted. For example, museums have received hundreds of letters which exclaim in astonishment that the portrait of Vermeer's

Girl With a Pearl Earring looks so much like a relative or friend. These admirers do not notice that the artist omitted significant details, such as the shape of her nose and the curve of her face, and even a clearly defined eye and hair color, which enable viewers to superimpose their own projections upon the canvas, thus prompting a deeper identification with the painting. The subtle illusions in Turner's *Slave Ship* inspired such deep identification that this painting alone vastly contributed to the abolishing of the slave trade in Britain. In the masterpieces of Rembrandt, some areas of the canvas necessarily require viewers to fill in the painting according to their life experience. Likewise in the sketches of Egon Scheile. Likewise in the last watercolors of Cezanne's *Mont Sainte-Victoire*. In the classic pen and ink drawings of Dante's *Inferno* by Gustave Doré, viewers may supply details of horror according to the emotional depth which they can imagine and psychically bear.

But how strikingly different did the study of images become with the invention of photography, which enables clear, concise images beyond the endurance of the viewer to be emblazoned upon the mind. No one at all familiar with the conflict in Vietnam will ever forget the little girl who runs screaming down a dirt road, her body burning with Napalm. The mighty fireballs exploding from the World Trade Center are forever seared upon our national consciousness, and no American, regardless of age, is immune from the horror inherent in the photo of the final shot which killed President John F. Kennedy.

As wrenching as many of these classic photographs inherently are, some of which literally altered forever the course of human history, how much more traumatizing are those *living* images which mercilessly intrude over the course of our lives from whose ruthless brutality we are afforded no psychic distance and therefore no means of psychic escape. Professional first responders, firefighters, and paramedics often suffer from the chronic stress of PTSD. For us laymen, one of those situations which cause such exquisite agony is to suddenly witness the suffering of a loved one behind a Trauma Room curtain, a shock of visual brutality for which we usually are unprepared.

Though I was prepared to witness the various machines, tubes, and assorted Emergency Room equipment, I had not been prepared to see my husband's disfigured face. Consequently, the scene I saw when standing with that physician at that curtain was seared upon my mind by the full force of shock for ten full months. I remembered how the doctor's left hand held the fabric, and how the folds appeared below his hand. I remembered the sound of the metal rings as he swept the curtain aside. Even the pattern of my husband's hospital gown was indelibly imprinted. Most symptoms of PTSD are intermittent flashbacks, which allow for merciful intervals of relief, but my nightmare was constant. For ten relentless months, I lived day and night at that curtain.

There was one aspect of that ordeal, however, for which I alone am totally responsible. I felt so insecure in my relationship with that physician and perceived such suspicion from his nursing staff, that standing at that curtain, I worried in an instant if he and his nurses would allow me to stay. After I ran to my husband and screamed into his ear, I forced myself to perform an act which, even at the time, I knew would scar me for life. I imagined that if I looked directly into my husband's eyes while continuing to speak to him with a voice unwavering, the staff would have no reason to escort me away. So I forced myself to do the most grisly act I hope I ever have to do while simultaneously maintaining a calm voice – I gazed at point-blank range directly into the eyes of death, ghastly yellow, streaked and pooled with blood – a horrible blank and lifeless stare which I remember to this day. For the gruesome impact of that isolated image, I alone am responsible. For the others, I simply was not forewarned.

Coupled with the scene in the Trauma Room, I also was subjected in the ICU to another image for which I was totally unprepared. Immediately after the nurses withdrew the life-support tubes, I got into bed with my husband, rested my head on his pillow and began to stroke him, assuring him that I would never leave, and that I would remain with him until he died. Almost immediately, he began to bleed. With my face only an inch away from his, blood began to stream from his mouth. I stifled my horror, because I understood that I was being challenged with the same dilemma I had faced only hours before in the Trauma Room. For the emotional sake of my children, who were still in various depths of shock, I had to remain calm, and for my husband, who even in his coma seemed to be able to hear, I had to remain reassuring. Maintaining that unwavering voice which I had perfected in the ER, I continued to whisper to him words of emotional and spiritual comfort, as I used tissue after tissue to wipe away his blood before tossing those tissues onto the floor. For the next two and one-half hours, I remained face to face with the man whom I had loved for fifty years, as I whispered to him while gently wiping away his blood. It was *solely* because of my intense love for him that I could bear such horror with any degree of emotional equanimity. After he died, as we were leaving the ICU, I turned around at the doorway and looked back at him for the last time. There, surrounding his bed like a carpet of red and pink blossoms, were the tissues I had used to wipe his blood from his face.

After my initial shock of seeing him bleed, and after realizing the importance of my maintaining emotional control, I welcomed the opportunity to minister to him with such selfless acts of tender devotion. But because I bore that shocking image only an inch away from my own face, coupled with all the other brutal shocks I received over those sixty hours, images for which I was given no merciful forewarning, it is no wonder that after his funeral, with my children still in disbelief and fair-weather friends abandoning me, my psyche collapsed into what is known in Central and South America as *soul loss*. 28

Primitive cultures regard soul loss, *susto,* to be a spiritual disease. It arises from a wrenching fright which shocks the central nervous system so profoundly that the soul is believed to flee in self-preservation, to literally leave the body because that environment is suddenly so disrupted. This robbing of one's fundamental life force, this stripping of

SARAH L. SEYMOUR-WINFIELD

one's essential *ch'ulel,* results in a psychic disintegration so utter that it feels internally to one's self and visually appears exteriorly to others that one has lost one's very core, one's very soul. If the brutality of the experience is of sufficient intensity, there is sometimes no hope that the individual can psychically reintegrate. 29

Though those hours in that hospital contained several brutal images, the initial psychic blows occurred at home. The shock of finding my husband on the floor was quickly followed by seeing the paramedics carry him out of the house, his face as white as snow. I shrieked at his deathly pallor. As they carried him out to the truck, my consciousness split, a process which the Central Americans would call the sudden separation of my soul from its hostile environment, or what psychology would term *profound dissociation.* My body ran aimlessly through the house as the EMT lights flashed on the walls of our living room and library, but my consciousness observed me run from high above the pasture across the road. Round and round through the front rooms, down the hall to the bedroom, then around to the front rooms again, I watched myself make circuit after circuit as lights flashed upon the walls, on our books, and onto the bricks of the fireplace from the truck still parked at the end of our drive.

I ran in shock until I realized that I was running *somewhere* – but where? Little by little, I realized that I was running *toward* – but toward where? Then in an abstraction which caused my brain to nearly explode, I had recollected enough deductive reasoning to know that I must *run* to the hospital by *driving a car.* I will never forget the sheer force of that abstraction, as though I had been viciously struck in the forehead – that the infinitive to *run* was the equivalent of the noun *car.* These shocks were followed in rapid succession by driving alone in the early morning darkness on icy roads, deliberately risking a head-on collision with a pickup, ramming my car into a snowbank in the ambulance bay, witnessing in utter innocence the horror behind the ER curtain, feeling the near-constant antipathy of the hospital staff, then watching my husband die as blood streamed from his mouth. This resulting depth of

102

susto could not be unlocked by three different psychotherapists, nor by a counselor at Hospice. The VA could offer nothing because I was not a veteran. I finally resorted to multiple treatments of EMDR to restore even the beginnings of psychic balance.

For their own protection, doctors and hospitals must become aware that in this current climate of legalism and blame, lawsuits filed for the infliction of PTSD are apparently becoming more common. A mother sued her obstetrician for failing to prepare her for the sight of her deformed infant, and her settlement was enormous. A PTSD website gives the example of a jury offering the plaintiff five hundred dollars per day in compensation. For the purposed length of the symptoms, the settlement was close to a third of a million dollars. The worst of my symptoms lasted three hundred days.

Even after two years, I still have generalized anxiety, startle easily, and am hyper-vigilant. Mercifully though, the nightmares of the ER and the ICU have largely disappeared. I am terrified to drive in any form of bad weather, and by extension, am afraid of storms. If I have an appointment scheduled for a day when the weather report promises snow or rain, I cancel, even if I have to pay for that missed appointment. Even the gentle showers of spring and fall whose sounds to most are soothing, cause me such suffering that my heart pounds and my hands shake. In an effort to heal myself, I took one insurance policy and bought a baby-grand piano, since I am a classically trained musician, but after only a few days, I played a piece of Rachmaninoff with such passion that I knocked the sound board completely out of position, so profound was my pain. When I was summoned for jury duty in the courthouse near that hospital, I wrote to the judge and asked to be excused because of chronic PTSD. Mercifully he relented.

If a catastrophe happens in surgery, the family is not present, but for those disasters inherent in either a trauma setting or an ICU, some assemblage of family will most likely be in attendance. In our situation, six of the nine adult members of our family were subjected to the same horror behind that ER curtain, and all nine were present in the ICU. Only one has ever spoken freely with me about what she experienced. All of them have established careers. If they had been the victims of the severity of PTSD which I had, or if I were not an independent writer whose schedule was entirely at my personal discretion, their careers would have been drastically impacted by the severity of their distress, and I would have been without income for ten months. Doctors, hospitals, and nurses as well need to protect themselves from lawsuits for punitive damages by formulating how best to compassionately prepare loved ones for the ghastly horrors awaiting them. Otherwise, brutal shocks such as the ones inflicted upon me, received by the innocent openness of the Child ego state, could force some to instinctively contact an attorney and strike back at the Parent professionals in sheer revenge.

After those ten bleak months of early grief, when my myopic self-absorption first began to broaden to include empathy for that attending physician, when my own individual ego states began to differentiate themselves from that whirl of undifferentiated white, it became abundantly clear that doctors themselves, as well as hospitals and their staffs, are actually fostering *Lottery Lawsuit* by providing the atmosphere in which opportunism can flourish. Opportunism nearly always arises from the powerful emotions of the Child ego state, those overwhelming passions which effectively disable discursive thought. Hospitals by their very nature are environments where strong emotions are perennially present. Opportunism thrives when the presence of these emotions makes it difficult for most to maintain rational perspective, or to maintain one's behavior as situationally appropriate, or to present one's character as behaviorally consistent. It thrives in those who sense great power, because their private thoughts and personal perspectives remain unchallenged and unchecked. In environments where relevant controls on escalating thoughts which can lead to abusive behavior are lacking, opportunism is likely to flourish.

This was the environment provided me during those final sixty hours, an expansive openness for my thoughts to have potentially escalated to the abusive and retaliatory. In terms of the three ego states, my hurting Child was offered no constructive guidance by any external nurturing Parent. There simply was no input provided from the exterior world which could have challenged my assumptions, or even actively reflected my emotions and thoughts. Everyone on that staff seemed to be hiding, as though everyone knew a secret except me.

The behavior of the Emergency Room professionals was inexplicable to me, an internal confusion which supported my original thesis that I should be cautious. I was totally oblivious to the fact that following that medical miscalculation, I possessed such extraordinary power, not only over that doctor because of his inadvertent mistake, but also over the hospital that employed him. Out of my awareness, the power differential had been dramatically inverted, the Parent/Child relationship which I had intuited at the hospital entrance abruptly reversed in my favor. Somehow I had advanced to Parent; somehow the staff had regressed to Child. After I witnessed the dire condition of my husband, I apparently was in total control. The abuse of power could very well have been mine, because I could have easily assumed the role of self-righteous Parent over and against that doctor, as well as over and against his hospital and staff, striking at everyone with a lawsuit because apparently, no one would have challenged me. The isolation implied in *See What You Made Me Do* provided me the perfect psychic void in which my own personal opportunistic tendencies could have expanded into the mercenary.

It was not until one year later that I understood that moment when, as our family was leaving the ER, I said *'Goodbye'* to the doctor. Because his face radiated toward me such inexplicable anxiety and dread, I'm imagining now that he expected me then to ask for the phone. He and I were at that intersection of *See What You Made Me Do* and *Now I've Got You,* that merciful interval when the hospital staff, for its own protection, could have dealt with me with compassionate persuasion to postpone a call to my attorney by providing me a comprehensive understanding of my husband's condition. But because neither the doctor nor any member of the staff had risked interacting with me throughout the preceding three hours, no one knew that there was no thought in this universe further from my mind than initiating a lawsuit. If during those hours I *had* been reflecting that I wanted to pursue a suit against that physician, the moment of the intersection of those two games would have been the hospital's opportunity to talk me down from that psychic ledge. However, given the permissive atmosphere in which my Child ego state was being provided free reign, where no external nurturing or critical Parent was offering me any guidance, that doctor would no doubt have handed me a phone, then provided me a phone book as well.

The crucial element conspicuously missing during those sixty hours is what was known to the ancient Greeks as *sunetos,* a depth of understanding in contrast to the superficial *dialogismoi* which, as the word implies, means the internal dialogue which everyone at every moment entertains within his own mind, a dialogue based solely upon one's own thoughts which perpetuate themselves without exterior input. This term comes from *dialogizomai* which means *reasoning back and forth.* These silent mental monologues are rooted in preconceived biases and confused preferential slants of the Parent and Child which are almost always rooted in the selfish, the narrow-minded, and the egotistical. These endless circlings of myopic thoughts calculate, plot, and skillfully reason but with insufficient data, the mind drawing conclusions which are far afield from what is real and what is inherently true. These incestuous internal monologues are effectively utilized to reinforce one's own prejudices as well as to support the prejudices of others. Contemporary psychology sometimes refers to this endless circling of self-absorbed thoughts as a *tape loop.* Verses in the Gospels which include *dialogismoi* refer to the evil thoughts which arise from one's own heart. 30

Dialogismoi stands in direct opposition to the expansive *sunetos,* which is derived from *syniemi,* which means *to understand by synthesizing* and *correlating facts and concepts.* It implies infused intelligence, prudent distinguishing, and discerning understanding. When used in the Gospels, *sunetos* references that wisdom which comes from a higher spiritual source, because human beings are creatures of spirit, and therefore are capable of expansive understanding.   31

Because the doctor and hospital were apparently so afraid that I would legally retaliate, and that because of their apprehension, I was left largely alone, the only thought process available to me in the absence of correct incoming information was the superficial *dialogismoi,* the endless thought loops which are always hopelessly flawed and lacking in synthesized understanding. Sometimes it seemed that I was trying to formulate a DNA strand in which two-thirds of the genes were missing. This desperate attempt to make medical sense from what was to me largely incomprehensible by using only my own myopic thought processes which are inherently biased and flawed, provided me the essential mental void where my innate opportunism could have flourished. I could have simply injected into my imagined genetic sequence what I as a layman assumed was appropriate, fantasizing that my strand of DNA spelled not *logical consequence,* but rather *medical malpractice.*   32

It appears that doctors and their hospitals have accepted as truth the superstitious belief that if they avoid the spouse and family, deny them the comprehensive understanding of *sunetos*, and abandon them to deal with their tragedy alone as best as they can, then the institution can magically prevent the loss of financial stability, the loss of reputation, and the tarnishing of the doctor's career. This tactic may indeed have worked on occasion, but such fairy-tale *dialoqismoi* is fundamentally self-destructive, because though the institution rightly maintains that the patient is its first priority, it was not my dying husband but I, his wife, who had the power to sue.   33

If I did not have above average intelligence and somewhat of an intellectual grasp on my husband's condition, if I had not understood that the consequence of the medical miscalculation was in fact one of the possibilities of his disease, if I had not evolved over six decades a capacity to maintain self-control and to delay judgment until a deeper understanding surfaced spontaneously, if I had encouraged my private thoughts and emotions to escalate in that environment where relevant controls were conspicuously lacking, if I had not been born with an innate loathing of taking advantage of another's misfortune, and if I at that time had felt the extraordinary extent of my power, then the final sum of my personal traumas as well as the medical error, added to the behavior of the hospital during those sixty hours, and coupled with the history of my husband's treatment during the preceding ten years, could have easily prompted my innate opportunism to expand into a merciless pursuit of not one lawsuit, but five.

It is not only the unfortunate *hamartia* of the physician which prompts opportunistic lawsuits, but also the negative emotions aroused in the perspective plaintiff over the course of treatment, and in my case, the emotions which could have been aroused in me by the behavior of the medical attendants during those final sixty hours. The pervasive silence of that hospital could have been interpreted by one hundred different potential plaintiffs in one hundred different ways. At that time of our crisis though, I read their emotional distance as burnout and self-protective professional detachment. Others however, who might have interpreted that emotional void as callousness, indifference, and even cruelty, could have utilized the medical error as fuel for a lawsuit of pure malevolent spite.

This vengeful dynamic is explored in the play *Twelve Angry Men*. The last juror to change his original vote from *guilty* to *not guilty* had been so emotionally traumatized decades before by his own son's hatred and callousness toward him, that the juror desperately wants to project his own agony onto the young defendant by voting in favor of lethal injection. The juror longs to play the ultimate form of *Now I've Got*

You, You Son of a Bitch, because the father had been destabilized in every way for decades from one significant event. Such blatant projection and transference are the last interior conflicts to be resolved in that beastly hot jury room filled with angry fictional men. However, in our world of reality, these same dynamics may be displayed in the plaintiff's pursuit of a vengeful lawsuit which uses one physician as the scapegoat, the unfortunate doctor who has destabilized the plaintiff's entire life as well as her entire system of belief by his medical error. She may plan to do unto him what he did unto her, and by extension, do unto the hospital as well what the staff did unto her.

In a fit of self-righteous retaliatory rage, she calls her attorney and asks his support as she initiates the prototypical game *Let's Destabilize the Doctor and His Hospital as They Destabilized Me.* If she phones from the Trauma Center, the game has already begun. Otherwise, it is the physician's reception of the summons which is the beginning of that process. The relationship between the doctor and his hospital is immediately disrupted, his professional relationships instantly strained with resentment and blame. His personal life with family and friends is destabilized as well, since he can discuss this immense emotional burden with no one except his attorney. As the lawsuit mercilessly progresses, the doctor's own practice becomes disrupted, because patients notice a strain in their favorite physician and worry if they should seek medical expertise elsewhere. The doctor must of necessity experience that destabilization even within his own person, because now he must behave as though he is half a man. His spontaneous Child must be consistently repressed, his true feelings rendered invisible by the wearing of his tragic mask. Bound by the dignity of his Oath to *do no harm*, he must present himself at all times as a Sunday School version of compliant adapted Child, because any public revelation of his true feelings could very well support that, at the time of the medical mistake, he truly was irresponsible.

In striking contrast however, the spontaneous Child of the plaintiff is free to indulge in her every whim. Lacking any internal supervision from her Parent ego state, and because her internal Adult is temporarily disabled by pain and possibly greed, she is backed by society's outrage and continuous approval that she toward the doctor has every right to level abuse. Her own life as well as her relationships thrive throughout this disaster, because she is viewed as the *victim,* the innocent victim for whom her attorney will eagerly *fight.* Witnessing the emotional, professional, and psychological wreckage in the life of the physician is welcomed by the irresponsible plaintiff as pure delight. Because her own grief and depression have been effectively postponed by all the legal uproar, she will most likely never wander aimlessly around her house in her nightgown with ties and suspenders draped around her neck. At the expense of the doctor and his hospital, she thrives as the center of society's attention. Though her case will undoubtedly be won by the physician, her original goal has been accomplished. Her doctor, both professionally as well as personally, is now fundamentally destabilized. He now doubts himself. And he knows as well that in all probability, almost of necessity, he will almost certainly make another mistake. His self-esteem, his professional confidence, as well as his respect in the eyes of his peers will never again be the same. The goal of the plaintiff has been achieved. She secretly does not care if the doctor is declared *not guilty,* because every plaintiff essentially wins every malpractice trial. She has destabilized her physician and his hospital as effectively as they destabilized her. That was her covert intent.

Arthur Miller wrote that his play *After the Fall* was *"about the human animal's unwillingness or inability to discover in himself the seeds of his own destruction."* These seeds of mutual destruction are increasingly apparent at this time in the United States, both within the medical profession and within patients and their families as well. The laity, doctors, and their hospitals have indulged in so many psychic games with each other for so long that we have achieved a deadly, mutually reinforcing homeostasis. 34

Everyone who plays a game enters with a psychic presupposition. Berne assures us that the very purpose of the game itself is to reinforce that, in an every-changing world, one's personal perspective is correct, and one's very self is stable. As a result of the predetermined stance of the medical community, which is based upon former experience, every patient and family has the potential to inflict substantial pain. Therefore physicians view loved ones like me as a threat, and view intelligent and highly functioning families like mine as worthy of suspicion. Regardless of observable incoming information, hospitals perpetuate their bias that families in crisis should be avoided. As a result of the predetermined stance of the laymen, which concludes from the sheer number of malpractice lawsuits that all physicians are increasingly incompetent, and hospitals are only interested in themselves, families now translate the detached professionalism and polite aloofness of doctors and hospital staff as either confirmation of guilt, or proof that the insularity of institutions is worthy of millions of dollars in retaliatory lawsuits. Even the benign behaviors my family displayed may have subconsciously reinforced a superstitious professional bias – that because our family did not sue, therefore the indifference of that hospital was appropriate. The suspicion of the professional Parent is fueling the outrage of the wounded Child, and the outrage of the wounded Child is perpetuating the suspicion of the professional Parent. Each predetermined stance is reinforcing the other's predetermined stance. It is these entrenched presuppositions which are perpetuating this deadly homeostasis.

In the meantime, clinics are closing, patients have died in ambulances because the nearest hospital had shut down, and high-risk mothers faced possible death for themselves and their unborn babies because their nearest maternity facility was closed. And still the game of *Lottery Lawsuit* remains a favorite national pastime, a supposedly respectable use of time, viewed as a responsible use of adult energy and personal resources to cannibalistically destroy the very profession vowed by compassion to guard our very lives.

Every adult in this country is guilty of perpetuating this medical malpractice crisis. Everyone without exception is complicit. I myself am guilty of playing with the ER doctor and staff the same games they played with me. The emotions of the staff seemed so fragile and so precariously balanced after witnessing the consequences of the miscalculation, that I literally was as afraid to interact with them as they were afraid to interact with me. Worried that they possessed the power to prevent me from remaining with my husband, I deliberately made no demands. Though my reason was lofty, both compassionate for the patient and protective of him as well, I was complicit nevertheless in playing the psychic games the staff of the hospital had introduced.

Judges are guilty of entertaining thousands of suits which they admit have neither legal nor moral merit. Attorneys are guilty of accepting illegitimate suits to enhance their bank accounts or further their careers. Medical schools are guilty of teaching generations of physicians that professional distance and cool observation of the family is the appropriate stance when dealing with loved ones overwhelmed by grief. Doctors and nurses are guilty of not adequately preparing, or not preparing at all, the psyches of loved ones to witness the horrors of terminal illness and dying. Clergy of all faiths are guilty of not preaching from pulpits that compassion, mercy, and forgiveness are responsible foundational responses to innocent medical error. All Americans are guilty of refusing to embrace the humanity of their physicians by insisting that, at all times and in every situation, doctors must display a professional ability which is superhuman and clearly unrealistic for all mortal men. This nation itself, the wealthiest in the world, is guilty of its strident greed and flagrant opportunism which feeds its insatiable appetite whenever medical errors arise. Families are guilty of selfishly perpetuating far beyond viability the lives of hopelessly ill loved ones to such extremes of fragility that any medical intervention, however mild, could easily result in a lawsuit. We laymen are guilty of not having the spiritual fortitude to bear our inevitable personal tragedies without inflicting retaliatory agonies upon others. The national government as well as legislatures of individual states are guilty of not providing families the means to receive appropriate compensation for those who truly are worthy, other than by attempting to publically destroy the reputation of the doctor as well as his career. And fundamentally, we are guilty of a lack of respect and gratitude for those who have dedicated hundreds of thousands of dollars as well as eight or more years in the learning of their skills, and who have endured many emotional and psychological trials while perfecting their art. *Lottery Lawsuit* perpetuates a spiral of violence for which this entire nation is accountable.

Guilt is never easy to confess. For both the professionals as well as for those patients and families they serve, this will not be an easy admission. The complicity which each side offers for the perpetuation of this deadly malpractice game will be even more shameful to acknowledge. But games, however deadly and however self-defeating, are perpetuated because both sides are deeply committed to their continuance, so that neither participant is forced to risk an open and loving stance.

Would society have said that I had a *right* to sue
that Emergency Room physician as well as his hospital?

Yes.

Would I have been able to find an attorney
who would fight to the death for me?

Undoubtedly.

Would I have left the legal arena
with a financial settlement?

Possibly.

But knowing the extenuating circumstances surrounding my husband's treatment during the preceding decade, and knowing other factors which quite possibly would have never been revealed during the process of litigation, I would have walked away from that courtroom seriously diminished in my own eyes, and I would never have been able to recapture my shattered self-respect.

03 80

The Open and Loving Stance

For where there is love of man there is also love of the art.

Hippocrates

Buckminster Fuller said that when he found a solution to a problem, if that solution was not beautiful, he knew it was intrinsically wrong. The solution which hospitals have discovered which supposedly eliminates or reduces the number of illegitimate lawsuits is obviously not only ineffective, it is not beautiful. If the deliberate neglect of spouses and families who could potentially sue actually impacted the number of mercenary lawsuits, then the deliberate avoidance of action by hospital personnel would be assessed as indeed both beneficial and correct. But since the professional stance I witnessed during my husband's final hours did not contribute in any way to my not filing a suit, then the solution assessed as prudent and wise was actually of no worth. More important, *vitally* important, is that this deliberate failure to emotionally and psychologically minister to spouses and families in the overwhelming throes of crisis actively suppresses the empathic response inherent in human nature. This conscious refusal to respond to one's own human heart is beneath our dignity as human beings, and is fundamentally in opposition to that compassion upon which the medical profession itself is nobly founded. It is this *intentional* suppression of compassionate love which shrinks the *unintentional* error of that Emergency Room physician to insignificance.

The Danish philosopher, Søren Kierkegaard, wrote that his readers can comb in vain the writings of the pagans of antiquity for a reference which even vaguely approximates the noble universal inherent in Christianity's *"You shall love your neighbor as yourself."* Though it is true that this New Testament commandment epitomizes the non-distinctive, impartial, non-preferential love which characterizes the heights of the Christian life, this very principle of selfless love is implied as well in the pre-Christian Oath of Hippocrates. Formulated in the pagan era of omnipotent gods and goddesses, when the Great Physician was Apollo, half-brother of Dionysus, and the entire Greek pantheon was evoked to ratify the covenant of each new doctor, the Oath nevertheless foreshadows the selfless love which by its very nature surges munificent and indifferent, toward any and all.

A contemporary update of this Oath was formulated by the Academic Dean of the School of Medicine at Tufts University during the same year in which Eric Berne published his *Games People Play*. Paraphrasing the original Oath, his modern version specifies –

I will remember that I do not treat a fever chart, a cancerous growth, but a sick human being, whose illness may affect the person's family and economic stability. My responsibility includes these related problems, if I am to care adequately for the sick...I will remember that I remain a member of society, with special obligations to all my fellow human beings, those sound of mind and body as well as the infirm. 35

What a blessing for our family if the sentiments of this contemporary revision were fully addressed to us during those final sixty hours, when our children were about to lose their father, and my solid, loving, devoted marriage was drawing to its close. What a blessing if the staff had remembered that my husband's fatal illness *affected our entire family,* and that the *related problem* of our response to the finality of our loss was one of the hospital's primary *responsibilities.* What a blessing for me to have felt like I too was *a member of the doctor's larger society,* and that my children and I who were *sound of mind and body* deserved the same solicitous care *as the infirm.* The ancient wisdom of non-discriminatory love which was first articulated two thousand years ago, and which was embodied by the students of Hippocrates five hundred years before, would then have been visibly witnessed as a living love in a hospital of today.

Those sixty hours, however, did include a few touching moments which strengthened my hope that the emotional trauma of families could be mercifully lessened by the compassionate concern offered them by the hospital staff, and that the number of vengeful lawsuits initiated by the furious Child against an indifferent Parent could be dramatically reduced. This inspiration began at the onset of that crisis.

My desperate call to the 911 dispatcher could very well serve as the prototype for the perfect dialogue with someone in the throes of panic and crisis, a standard worthy of study in psychology books. After the dispatcher extracted enough information from me to send the EMT truck to our address, and after ascertaining that my husband was still breathing, she immediately switched from her Adult ego state into her nurturing Parent as she comforted me as a panicked Child. Over and over she encouraged me to *"Stay on the phone with me. You hear me? You keep talking to me, and don't hang up."* Every few seconds she switched back into her Adult to ask, *"Do you see them coming?"* When I responded *"No,"* she once again returned to her nurturing Parent, reassuring me that the medics were on their way. Her voice was firm, directive, simultaneously comforting, conveying to me at all times that, even though I knew my world was falling apart, she knew everything was under control. When I eventually screamed into the phone, *"I see lights!"* she lovingly responded, *"Good luck to you and your husband,"* and hung up. Our conversation, which took less than two minutes, though it seemed to me to take hours, was the perfect interaction in a crisis. Every vector in our transaction was a straight line. No lines of communication were crossed. Her Adult was to my Adult, and her Parent was to my Child. The meta-communication from me to her was *'Please stay with me,'* and from her to me was *'I will.'* Because our dialogue included no manipulation and no deceit, I felt absolutely safe during the interim between finding my husband on the floor until the arrival of the paramedics. She had instantly aroused in me a profound trust.

During the last day of my husband's life, a cafeteria worker brought me a tray, then later came to retrieve it. I commented that I liked the coleslaw. Much to my surprise, he reappeared one hour later with a sheet of typing paper upon which was printed in oversized print the coleslaw recipe of that hospital. Though it no doubt appeared to those overhearing our interaction that I was giving exaggerated praise for the inconsequential, I was actually extending profuse gratitude to him for treating me as a human being. During the most painful and devastating hours of my life, he had treated me with kindness. Compassion and basic kindness had appeared.

During the final morning of my husband's life, I had a brief conversation with an ICU nurse. Later that afternoon she explained that she was scheduled to withdraw life-support that evening, but that after meeting me, she emotionally could not do it. So she asked another to replace her. She assured me that she herself would be present, but would not participate in the procedure herself. When the tubes were actually withdrawn, I stood by the bed while everyone else in our family remained outside. I felt someone's arm around my shoulder with such a firm grip that the hand seemed to penetrate down to my bone. I'm guessing it was the nurse with whom I had spoken that afternoon. Just as she had promised, she had been there for me.

A short while before support was withdrawn, another nurse approached to give my husband an injection. When I noticed that her hands were shaking, I held her hands in mine. She said that the mixture was *"so delicate,"* that if she *"got it wrong,"* it would *"kill him."* I answered, *"My husband could very well die soon anyway. If you got it wrong, that's all right."* I so appreciated those tender moments of touching emotional intimacy. Such brief intervals of kindness enabled me not to feel alone.

Following my husband's death, I desperately needed to put some semblance of closure on a crisis which, at that time, seemed it had left me permanently traumatized. I sought *sunetos* to replace my endless recyclings of *dialogismoi.* I needed answers to questions regarding the horrors I witnessed as my husband was dying, and an understanding of what had transpired in the ICU. In a sense, I needed those essential, imaginary genes which I could then insert into my flawed imaginary strand of DNA so that the entire ordeal made sense. But to gain that understanding, I did not want to interface then with my husband's primary physicians, and I was reticent as well to ask that particular hospital. Luckily I stumbled upon a website run by three physicians in a clinic in India, who answered health questions emailed to them from all over the world. The doctors responded using concise medical terminology, then explained each term in words I could easily understand. Each physician was forthright, extremely polite, and mercifully compassionate as well about what I had lived through during my husband's last few months. All transactions were straight, and no vectors crossed. One of them was so concerned about the burden I had borne largely alone that he gave me his private email address to use whenever I could no longer bear my loss. I am enormously grateful to all three and to their practice, and for their sending me, when I needed it the most, such gracious and sincere support from half a world away.

After several emails, our relationship spontaneously ended, because they had granted me a deep *sunetos*, a broad, synthesized understanding. My fantasized DNA strand was then as complete as I needed it to be. It was because of the patience and clarity those doctors conveyed while providing me the information I desperately needed during those ten months of grief and silent introspection, that my belief about that Emergency Room physician was reinforced – there indeed was no cause for me to sue for medical malpractice. Such honest, enlightened, and comforting displays of basic humanity from one of the poorest countries in the world. Our brief relationship was charged with absolute confidence and infused with peace, conveying to me that elemental love of neighbor which is the hallmark of the truest form of adult life all around this globe.

My daughter and I now wish that we had experienced a similar pattern of sincere game-free communication with the professionals who met us at the entrance to the Trauma Center. The atmosphere which the 911 dispatcher created could be easily transplanted into the hospital setting by inserting the one essential transaction which was so apparent in my dialogue with the dispatcher but which was so conspicuous by its absence in the hospital – *the nurturing Parent acknowledging the scared Child.* The insertion of only one or two sentences using the following mode would have inspired in us both instant trust – *the dispassionate reflection of our affect.* The nurse could have said to my daughter, *'Oh good, you're here. Your mother just arrived. I see that you are worried about your father. I assume you understand what is wrong with him?'* Or the doctor could have said, *'I'm Dr. X. I've been attending your husband. I can see that you are scared for him, because it is obvious that he has been ill for a long, long time.'* Though these statements from both professionals would have undoubtedly prompted momentary tears, my daughter and I nevertheless would have then been able to quickly access our Adult, because our Child would have felt recognized and supported. That simple recognition of our affects, requiring less than thirty seconds, would have established an atmosphere between us and the staff of equality and mutual respect. One or two short sentences would have established between strangers an instantaneous trust. In a medical crisis, those precious thirty seconds may be all the time one has.

How wonderful for me if I had been met at the door with the following affirmation. Rather than sensing, *'Oh no, his wife is here,'* how supportive for me to have intuited, *'Thank God his wife is here! Of the billions of people on this planet, only her touch can assure him now. Of all the voices on this planet, her voice is the only one he is desperate to hear. She can now provide our patient what our staff necessarily cannot. Thank God his wife is here.'* How empowering for me to have intuited that. Even more empowering to have actually heard that! How strengthening for my daughter also if that nurse had empowered her to stay strong for me. Though neither of us actually *needed* to hear such remarks, because we understood that his condition was dire and his future bleak, those comments nevertheless would have enabled us both to feel like **valuable members of the hospital team, rather than enemies of the staff.** Meeting us at the door with empowerment would have set a beautiful precedent for a trust which would have sustained us both throughout the coming hours.

Apparently hospitals assume that if communication flows solely on the information level, the feelings of the family will not have to be dealt with by the staff. Though this practice truly does provide the hospital a short-term gain, it unfortunately provides as well a long-term disadvantage. The pain felt by families in medical crisis must be acknowledged by the *nurturing Parent of the staff, not overlooked by their Adult.* Without this simple recognition of affect, the family's private pain is exacerbated by implied public condescension, both felt within the Child ego state. If the pain of that subtle humiliation is allowed to escalate, the Child may eventually lash out at the hospital's indifferent Parent by leveling at the doctor and his institution a vengeful lawsuit which uses medical error as opportunistic.

The gene for opportunism which I and everyone on this planet innately possess as an essential component of human DNA, a genetic sequence which affords the individual as well as the entire species a means of physical survival, was displayed in my own behavior during those final hours. The very word *opportunism* is derived from the Latin *ob portus,* a contraction which means either *toward the harbor or entrance,* or *facing the harbor or entrance.* How poignant this term becomes when applied to my circumstances, since my husband was facing the entrance to death, and I myself was simultaneously facing that stage of life when I would be forced to live and die without him. Though the ER doctor and hospital administration apparently expected me to direct that gene toward the pursuit of a vengeful lawsuit with the hope of receiving a sizeable financial settlement due to that medical miscalculation, my innate opportunism was directed instead toward infusing my husband's dying and actual death with as much beauty, dignity, and respect as I could manage in the sterile environment of a Trauma Room as well as among the machines, tubes, and inexplicable equipment of Intensive Care.

While driving to the hospital, I reasoned that his death would necessarily happen only once. Only once would I be afforded this opportunity to minister to him at the end of his life. History would provide me no second chance, no occasion to regroup and try again, no means to undo and graciously redo what would inevitably take place only once. This realization infused into me a determination to do whatever the hospital demanded of me which would enable me to remain with my husband until he died. In a sense, I was committed to serving as his midwife as he was born into the ethereal realms of pure spirit. I was also determined to take every advantage to make memories for my children which they could treasure for the remainder of their lives. During the drive through that blinding snow, I set my two intentions in stone, carved them in rock. I would remain with my husband at all costs to provide him a beautiful farewell from our marriage and from this world, and to the maximum degree of my strength, would create as many beautiful scenes as I could as a lasting legacy to me and to our family. By the time I arrived at the hospital, my gene for opportunism had been activated.

When I realized that the staff seemed intent on leaving me alone, I spent hour after uninterrupted hour with my husband, speaking softly to him, hoping against hope that in his coma he could hear me and understand. When I saw that my children as well were sunk so deep into shock that they were emotionally unable to speak directly to their father whose appearance was so ghastly, I realized that, within reasonable limits, I had extraordinary power over my husband's dying process. I would not have to relate to the hospital staff, neither would I have to compete with anyone for time alone with him. Adapting with flexibility to these unexpected dynamics which were so contrary to my expectations, I took advantage of the situation out of purely self-interested motives. I would capitalize on the aloof demeanor of the staff, capitalize on what seemed to me to be their empathic errors, and utilize the distraction of the hospital to my own and my husband's advantage. Because I understood that apparently I would not be forced to interact with strangers, I was in the privileged position to devote the final hours of our marriage solely to him.

During his previous hospitalizations when friends came to visit, my husband and I participated in casual conversations which were sometimes serious but most often humorous. These dialogues were obvious attempts to keep up his spirits as well as my own. During this final hospitalization, however, when those same people were either emotionally or psychically unable to engage with a man who appeared to be a corpse, I took advantage of their reluctance by devoting more time to him myself. I rationalized that rather than waste precious minutes encouraging adults to bravely engage with a man whose appearance was so ghastly, instead I would devote that time to actually comforting and assuring him myself. Any oversights which my children and others could have perceived in my attitude which was totally riveted upon him, I would sensitively deal with later. Those last precious hours were not the appropriate time. When one did ask for private time alone with my husband, I generously granted that interval and quietly left the room, but when no one else requested such privacy, I considered those hours as mine. In a sense, I was compromising in sheer opportunism a principle which I formerly held as primary – that everyone without exception should be included. But under the circumstances of a man who was dying, I refused to engage in those social pleasantries which would have made those visitors more comfortable. Instead, I disregarded that former value and ministered to him myself.

Within hours if not within minutes, I was to lose what I had profoundly treasured since I was a shy sixteen. In the sense of the purely opportunistic, I understood that I had nothing further to lose. I made requests of the ICU staff for my own benefit and for the benefit of my children's memories, because the pay-off of the nurses granting those requests would be greater than the penalty of their saying 'No.' I asked if my children could bring from our house my husband's favorite afghan which I had recently knit, his favorite photographs, and other assorted items which he valued, including a painting which had been in the room where his mother died, as well as a photo of his father. The nurses gave their gracious consent. When a gorgeous pink azalea arrived from friends in Michigan, I asked the nurses if it could remain beside his bed. Since our home is filled with houseplants, I thought that plant would comfort both my children and me. Though such a request is usually denied in the ICU, the nurses graciously granted their permission. When I noticed that only one other patient was being cared for that evening, I took advantage of the nurses' light work load and asked if I could spend the last night of our marriage in bed with him. They gave me permission, thus enabling me to acquire a memory which I will always treasure. At the moment of his death, a photo was taken of him and me, our heads sharing the same pillow, snuggling under his favorite afghan.

My behavior during those sixty hours displayed the classic components of opportunism – the basic ability to make choices, to decide on a course of action most advantageous to one's self, to exercise self-motivation, to make external one's inner direction, to display creative inventiveness, and within the confines of an alien environment, to exercise personal freedom. Such behaviors displayed the positive aspects of healthy opportunism.

That same institutional environment, however, could have easily supported the dark, negative aspects of sadistic opportunism, whose expression would have been unhealthy for me and dangerously detrimental for that physician as well as his hospital. Opportunism thrives in the absence of external controls upon one's behavior, and flourishes in situations of crisis where relevant information is lacking. I was obviously in an environment where controls were lacking, because of the hospital's reticence to directly engage with me. I also was not granted a full understanding of my husband's condition, both because of the reluctance of the professionals to divulge information, as well as my own fear to inquire. Notable gaps were conspicuous in my fantasized strand of DNA. Fortunately I understood the essentials - that my husband was dying, that only hours remained in our marriage, and therefore the answers to my questions were, at that time, irrelevant. Such information could easily be obtained later. The psychic void in which our family spent those sixty hours was advantageous for me and for my children, but was that void advantageous for the Emergency Room physician and for his hospital? Only one ego state is qualified to answer that question, the state which Eric Berne calls the *Emancipated Adult.*

The medical profession as a whole is necessarily rooted in the Parent ego state. Consequently, its institutions are locked in the Parent as well. This psychic stance is actively taught and passed down from the elder medical Parent to the next generation of medical Parents, from Hippocrates to the present day. On the other hand, we laymen caught in the throes of medical crisis are necessarily locked within our scared and hurting Child. During my husband's final hours, it was this simple alternation and abrupt reversal from Parent to Child which was conspicuous. I entered the hospital as a panicked little girl, with the doctor in the Parent role, but when I left that Emergency Room hours later, I somehow had advanced to Parent, and the staff had regressed to scared Child. The same dynamic was played, but from the opposite direction. ***Our dominate ego states had reversed; they had not evolved.*** Throughout those hours, neither the professionals nor I had progressed beyond the Parent/Child paradigm. The ego state conspicuously absent throughout that ordeal was the Emancipated Adult.

Only the Liberated Adult is free to thoughtfully examine the stance of one's own internal Parent and Child ego states. Only the Adult is qualified to dispassionately examine, judge, accept as truth, or reject as falsehood the Parent attitudes handed down during childhood's impressionable years. In terms of individual physicians and medical institutions who routinely face the possibility of medical malpractice litigation, only the Adult of each physician can observe, evaluate, and comment upon his own beliefs lodged in his own Parent ego state which were imprinted upon him during his years of medical education, and only the Liberated Adult of his hospital administration is qualified to accept or reject the behaviors and attitudes which have been handed down to them from elder medical professionals as substantial truth. The Liberated Adult, the Emancipated Adult is free to accept or reject the attitudes and prejudices transmitted from the Parent ego state of the medical institution to the next generation of Parent professionals.

The past intrudes into our present through the imposed attitudes of our Parent, and the juvenile responses of our Child to those Parent maxims. However, one's internal Adult is the ego state which possesses the authority to temporarily disable one's existing Parent and Child so that a clinical, objective evaluation can be made of our historic present. The Fully Functioning Adult thus exercises great responsibility, not the flashy, self-righteous power wielding of the Parent, nor the self-indulgent temper tantrums of the rebellious Child, but rather the sanguine evaluation of each situation, the clinical analysis of whether the dynamics involved are workable for all. The Navy psychiatrist, Dr. Thomas A. Harris, student of Eric Berne noted, *(T)he revolutionary impact of the most revered religious leaders was directly the result of their courage to examine Parent institutions and proceed, with the Adult, in search of truth.* Though this observation was made in regard to the Church, this same observation can be addressed to the Parent medical establishment. 36

Attempting to objectively view those sixty hours through the clinical dispassionate analysis of my own Adult, it seems to me that though the freedom I was granted was advantageous for me and my children, and beneficial for my individualized care of my husband, the hospital's permissive stance toward me plus the hospital's ignorance of the state of my adult children was not advantageous for either the unfortunate doctor or for the institution itself. Because of their global refusal to interact with me and refusal to embrace even rudimentary eye contact, only two ICU nurses and one cafeteria worker possessed some awareness of my internal state. Basically no one knew my character. Their predominant means of judgment would necessarily have been based not upon direct, sincere communication, but rather upon the observation of my body language and other non-verbals. In consequence, when our family left the ICU, no one knew if I would sue. Without daring that essential face-to-face contact which would have assured the staff that I was no legal threat, the only option for the unfortunate doctor was to either wait for the summons which never materialized, or for him and his hospital to wait anxiously for the statute of limitations for our particular state to mercifully expire. The only assurance to which that ER physician and his staff must have desperately clung was that, standing at the door to the ER office, I said 'Goodbye' to him rather than 'I'll see you in court.' Such utter submission to a layman struggling through the worst crisis of her life! Such utter resignation, such pathetic passivity to a woman who did not have all the pertinent facts! It is not only the selfish opportunism of the laity, but also this shocking lack of healthy opportunism in the professional community which is fueling the current medical malpractice crisis.

Since I as the wife of the patient had the power to sue, it would have been wisely opportunistic for both the staff of the Trauma Center as well as the staff of the ICU to have dared to engage with me at periodic intervals, to have risked initiating diminutive conversations of two or at most three sentences during which the professionals could have assessed how I was responding to my husband's ghastly appearance and to his obviously fatal condition, and gauged as well the responses of our grown children. If I had requested information, it could have been presented in the simplest layman's terms filtered always through the nurturing Parent of the staff, rather than harshly presented in the clinical terminology of their Adult. Such information which I acquired later through the doctors in India would have been too aggressively brutal to emotionally assimilate during the actual crisis, but the general description of my husband's condition would have been bearable, if I had requested it. Witnessing how well I bore the weight of that information would have provided the hospital valuable insight into my character.

The hours we spent in the Trauma Center provided many opportunities for such miniature conversations. Several short contacts with that attending physician would have fostered a trust in him which, during the crisis, I truly did not feel, and would have mercifully inspired in him as well an elemental trust in me. Since I was in the hospital for most of those sixty hours, my presence could have been viewed as mercifully opportunistic for the staff, providing a minimum of forty waking hours during which numerous diminutive dialogues could have taken place which assessed my predilection to sue. These miniature conversations could have been considered *emotional temperature checks* or *psychological blood pressure checks,* periodic readings of my personal pain level to assess if I, as the potential plaintiff, seemed to be a legal risk. Even if it is discovered that a potential plaintiff is contemplating a lawsuit, the positive aspects of opportunism, studied and internalized by the hospital staff, could be utilized to de-escalate a potential plaintiff away from a mercenary pursuit.

Both healthy and destructive opportunism necessarily imply the innate ability to assess one's situation, to be instantly flexible to incoming information, to spontaneously alter one's course of action toward a perceived good, and to foresee somewhat the consequences of one's actions, even if those actions are only self-serving. Both healthy and sadistic opportunism imply the ability to make one's own choices, to attempt to steer one's fate, to pursue a course of action based upon a sense of inner direction and purpose, and to make creative and inventive decisions. Both types require insight and discernment, and necessarily demand a deep sense of self-motivation. Since strong initiative is required to sustain a vindictive lawsuit, the hospital staff could redirect that energy into the family's deeper understanding of the medical crisis, into a more extensive appreciation of the medical situation, and as a result, into an alternate expression of free choice. Since all opportunists, both healthy and sadistic, value personal freedom, the alternative expression of that personal independence could be presented as a wise and viable choice. Such direct intervention, though, requires that the hospital staff boldly face what it most profoundly fears – the loved one.

Such brief interactions would have been not only favorable for the hospital to ascertain if I were or were not a threat, but these miniature encounters would have assured me and my children as well that we were considered important, that our family too was one of the hospital's *responsibilities*, that we too were members of the doctor's larger *society*, and that we too who were *sound of mind and body* deserved the same solicitous care as *the infirm*. I could have been mercifully forewarned about what I was inevitably to witness and compassionately prepared for what I would of necessity be forced to bear. The ancient wisdom and caring concern of Hippocrates would have been in evidence in the contemporary world within my own life. 37

Instead, I witnessed a lack of professional self-confidence, a fundamental uncertainty and fear, a failure of personal engagement, and an avoidance of human contact. In this age of psychology, when non-verbals are widely known and analyzed, when we laymen understand the subtle implications of the unspoken and the unexpressed, I could have easily interpreted the hospital's dis-ease with me as an open confession of guilt. It was not my behavior during that crisis which aroused such pervasive suspicion, but rather the mental attitudes and psychological assumptions inherited through the professional Parent fueled and exacerbated by the fears of the professional Child which led to the anxiety about me felt within the staff, and which led to the resulting anxiety toward them felt within me. Examining those professional attitudes to ascertain if they truly are beneficial, and if they truly do diminish lawsuits which are destroying the very profession vowed to compassionately care, will require the cool, academic, dispassionate discernment of the medical profession's Emancipated Adult, will require raw courage and daring, will demand that the institution suspend its predetermined stance that families like mine are liabilities, and wives like me are threats.

Only two adjustments would be required in hospital policy – 1) the professional Parent to verbally reflect the frightened affect of incoming families for the purpose of inspiring instantaneous trust, and 2) the staff to periodically relate to loved ones out of both compassion and self-protection for the purpose of forming a rudimentary bond. Minor changes. But these will not be experienced by the medical establishment as minor adaptations, but rather as substantial professional risks. However, it is precisely this daring to face those who can potentially sue which will lead to the reduction of mercenary lawsuits by radiating toward all who enter those soaring Trauma Center doors the non-discriminatory love about which Hippocrates wrote so long ago. *Daring* to confidently address those who now are fundamentally feared, *daring* to courageously risk what was once considered the ultimate professional danger, *daring* to address those tsunamis of passion in the hearts of loved ones overwhelmed by grief, will dramatically impact the current crisis in medical malpractice by making each interaction between the profession and the grieving family not only advantageous for the hospital staff, but also by creating an awareness in the family that doctors and nurses are ultimately performing their arduous and relentless responsibilities not as mere requirements of their profession, but rather as works of selfless, merciful, and compassionate love.

CB EO

Hippocrates Today

Submit. In agony learn wisdom.

Aeschylus
Prometheus Bound

My husband's legacy to me includes precious children, priceless memories, as well as a grand library of great books. As a scholar of both ancient Greek and Hebrew, some of his most prized volumes, and some of the heaviest, contain not a single word of English. Despite his many patient attempts to introduce me to the mysterious depths of meaning inherent in these languages, the unintelligible squiggles of both alphabets eluded my comprehension throughout our marriage. I studied the masterpieces of the great tragedians in English, while he read them in Greek. He left to me his *Loeb Series of Classical Writings*, which appear in the original language on the left hand page with the English translation on the right. Four of those volumes written in both English and Greek are the *Writings of Hippocrates.*

Physicians in the era of Hippocrates brought into the gravity of each medical crisis little more than an observant eye, a compassionate heart, the wisdom of patience, and a great deal of hope. It was an era before microbiology, biochemistry, pathology, and all the other fields of knowledge whose pursuit drives medical students today to the brink of academic despair. Hippocrates organized disease according to a collection of symptoms, not according to a firm diagnosis. There were those symptoms which were contagious, and those which were not. There were those which were acute, and those which were not. Some diseases were named, but their classifications so commonly understood today were largely unknown. The skill of the physician was viewed primarily as assisting Nature itself to bring about healing, and to alleviate pain in so far as he could. In the age before anesthetics, however, this aspect of medicine alone was a supreme challenge. The guiding principle of this doctor, Hippocrates the Great, was the same as the guiding principle of his professional descendants today – *to help, or at least to do no harm.* 38

Medical bags then contained little more than bandages and herbs. Fevers were determined solely by touch, and pulse rate was not even recorded. Sound medical advice was the designation of the most advantageous times to eat *gruel*, the recommendation to wash *with soap that is warm*, and to drink from springs *whose source face the risings of the sun.* In a heart-breaking record of an adolescent overtaken by an epidemic, Hippocrates notes the gruesome symptoms of his patient over the course of three weeks. Then, using that emotional withdrawal employed by the greatest masters of fiction, that sudden emotional abandonment of the reader which is guaranteed to elicit from the heart of that reader the deepest response, Hippocrates states with a simplicity which even after twenty-five hundred years still merits tears: *Twenty-fourth day. Death.* 39

Originally, all the individual treatises presented in my four volumes were assumed to have been written by this master physician. Now scholars who detect such differences in style and viewpoint among those articles presume that Hippocrates did not write all these works, and even suggest that he wrote none at all. But while I recently studied those various manuscripts for the purpose of writing this chapter, I liked to imagine that all the disparate viewpoints were indeed the various perspectives of one man, because so many of his thoughts can be applied to the contemporary world as well as to my husband's own experience.

In an era when medical treatment was primitive and relied more on morale and positive thoughts than strict medical expertise, Hippocrates still cautioned his students that unfortunately, they may make an error in judgment, and personally hopes that they will accomplish *(their) cures easily without making a mistake.* Even when knowledge of healing was so minimal and so meager, physicians nevertheless worried about committing tragic errors. He even comments *that the physician who makes only small mistakes would win (his) hearty praise.* In our age, however, when thousands of drugs are available, and the number of possible drug interactions approach the speed of light, a physician in this twenty-first century is expected to never make a mistake, to never make a miscalculation, to never embody a human *hamartia,* or else we, his patients and families will threaten his reputation as well as his career with possible destruction and guaranteed shame. 40

Hippocrates also writes about the ingratitude of his patients and families who either take him for granted or make dismissive remarks about his compassionate care, a comment as relevant today as it was two and one-half millennia ago.

It is conceded that of those treated by medicine some are healed. But because not all are healed the art is blamed, and those who malign it, because there are some who succumb to diseases, assert that those who escape do so through luck and not through the art.

41

I was amazed to find so much material which applied not only to my husband's individual misfortune, but also to the current climate in which so many hold their physicians personally responsible for every conceivable stroke of fate. Apparently an equivalent of irresponsible claims for medical malpractice existed even in Hippocrates' day.

I wonder what adequate reasons induce them to hold innocent the ill-luck of the victims, and to put all the blame upon the intelligence of those who practice the art of medicine.

42

Hippocrates could very well have been envisioning the organized chaos of our contemporary Trauma Rooms where in the crisis of Code Blue, or in the desperate impasse of patients who, like my husband, were Dead on Arrival, the ensuing turmoil resulted in the catastrophic.

Time is that wherein there is opportunity, and opportunity is that wherein there is no great time...Whenever therefore a man suffers from an ill which is too strong for the means at the disposal of medicine, he surely must not even expect that it can be overcome by medicine... For when a diseased condition is stubborn and the evil grows, in the perplexity of the moment most things go wrong.

43

He even teaches us that those who encounter horrors such as those which I witnessed, images which are still prominent in my mind, are the same images which physicians in ancient Greece as well as contemporary experts in emergency medicine witness every day. Hippocrates assures us that all could very likely, to varying depths and intensities, suffer from the unique symptoms of PTSD.

For the medical man sees terrible sights, touches unpleasant things, and the misfortunes of others bring a harvest of sorrows that are peculiarly his.   44

How reassuring for me as a widow to read the writings of Hippocrates, to realize that my husband suffered *from an ill which (was) too strong for the means at the disposal of medicine,* and that I myself was reasonable to *not even expect that it (could) be overcome by medicine.* I was comforted also to read that in a crisis setting both in the ancient world as well as now, *opportunity is that wherein there is no great time,* and that often, sadly, *in the perplexity of the moment most things go wrong.* My husband's very psychic stance was also mentioned in the writings of this noble physician, because he was a man *not in love with death, but powerless to endure.* Even now, after two years, those words bring tears to my eyes. And how consoling also to realize that my torment of PTSD was a common professional hazard in the ancient world as well as now, and that both my husband's attending physician as well as I no doubt suffered many of the same memories.   45

My husband died because it simply was his time to die. Like that little boy shortly before the American Civil War, it simply was his time to die. What happened had been *prepared for (him) from all eternity; and the implication of causes was, from eternity, spinning the thread of (his) being, and of that which (was) incident to it.* The span of his life affirmed eternity's *conception of an hour.* I look now upon his sufferings, his disease, the medical miscalculation, as well as his death as all lovingly written by *the finger of God.* My understanding of that tragedy is living proof that we are all mysterious amalgams of the mortal and the divine. All of us, without exception, are capable of breathing rarified air at that dizzying stratospheric height *where the psychology of Man mingles with the psychology of God.*   46

CB ᙡ

August 27, 1883

Courage consists not in hazarding without fear,
but being resolutely minded in a just cause.

Plutarch

One of the most celebrated and recognizable images in Western art is *The Scream* by Edvard Munch.   It depicts a hairless, sexless figure poised with his hands on either side of his anguished face, standing upon a bridge over swirling seas beneath a tormented fiery orange-red sky. He utters a primal scream. Existentialists support that this canvas depicts modern man's fundamental *angst*, a despair essentially screamed by those who live in a world which was all but destroyed by two global wars, innumerable conflicts, and devastating atomic explosions.   Some believe it references the specific site which the painting depicts, a locale in close proximity to both a slaughterhouse and the insane asylum where the sister of the artist was a patient. Some imagine it is related to the Peruvian mummy which the artist might possibly have studied during the *1889 Exposition Universelle* in Paris. The mummy which had been buried in the fetal position, its hands alongside its face, seems to have also inspired one of the figures in the famous painting of Paul Gauguin, *Where Do We Come From? What Are We? Where Are We Going?* The painting of Munch has also been used as a symbol for the facial pain of *trigeminal neuralgia,* which has been described by its sufferers as one the most painful medical conditions.   But whatever the personal interpretation of this horrific enigmatic image, its true title is *Der Schrei der Natur,* or *The Scream of Nature.* Munch wrote of an experience -

'I was walking down the road with two friends when the sun set; suddenly, the sky turned as red as blood. I stopped and leaned against the fence, feeling unspeakably tired. Tongues of fire and blood stretched over the bluish black fjord. My friends went on walking, while I lagged behind, shivering with fear. Then I heard the enormous, infinite scream of nature.'

He explained later that at that time, *'I was stretched to the limit – nature was screaming in my blood...After that I gave up hope ever of being able to love again.'* 47

The painting itself seems to reference that private spiritual experience, but the lurid skies and turbulent waters are reminiscent of a catastrophic event which occurred when the artist was only twenty years old, a volcanic eruption of such colossal proportions that millions of people heard the planet itself utter a primal scream.

Krakatoa was an island midway between Java and Sumatra in the Sunda Strait which joins the Indian Ocean with the South China Sea. Three months before the final paroxysm, strange phenomena were observed and felt in the sea and the atmosphere itself. Just after midnight on the morning of May 10, a lighthouse keeper stationed at the southeastern entrance to the Strait saw the sea suddenly turn white in the night, its surface suddenly as flat as a shimmering mirror, the waters shivering slightly. Simultaneously, the lighthouse seemed to shift upon its foundation as a mysterious atmospheric tremor destabilized the sea and the very air itself. Five days later, similar phenomena were experienced with stronger and more sustained power over greater distances on either side of the Strait. Windows of shops shattered inexplicably; gas lights mysteriously dimmed; the ball of the astronomical clock suddenly shuddered to a full stop. It is now understood that these enigmatic occurrences are the ominous portents of an impending volcanic eruption. Disastrously unfortunate for those immediately involved, European ships found themselves stranded in those now famous waters during the hours immediately preceding that volcano's ultimate destruction on August 27, 1883, its explosion on that infamous Monday morning of such ferocity, it has been termed *the crack of doom.* The records of those courageous men transform Dante's literary descent into his literary *Inferno* into an infernal reality, a monumentally malicious moment when the majesty of the epic and the horror of the historic met. [48]

By five p.m. that Sunday afternoon before the volcano's ultimate detonation, a profound darkness had engulfed the entire length of the Java coast. European ships stranded in that Strait were bombarded by the fiery hail of pumice still warm from the infernal furnace in which it had been forged. One ship positioned only ten miles from the volcano, found itself navigating aimlessly in a blinding late-afternoon night, the captain and his crew covering the ship's skylights to preserve the glass and protecting themselves from burns with boots and coats.

The night was a fearful one; the blinding fall of sand and stones, the intense blackness above and around us, broken only by the incessant glare of varied kinds of lightning, and the continued explosive roars of Krakatoa made our situation a truly awful one.

49

Six hours later, the crew peered through the darkness until the convulsive island loomed visible and observed *chains of fire* ascending and descending between the mountain and the sky while simultaneously to the southwest continually rolled *balls of white fire.* By midnight, the darkness had doubly intensified, the mountain roaring, hot winds choking the crew with the smell of burning sulfur, raining cinders impacting them with the searing burns of iron, the atmosphere one moment *intensely black, the next a blaze of light.* They witnessed their ship ominously engulfed in those electrical clouds which are known to terrified sailors as St. Elmo's fire, *a peculiar pink flame...from fleecy clouds which seemed to touch the mast-head and the yard-arms,* electrifying the ship and all its rigging with eerie phosphorescence. 50

The following morning, the ship had mercifully sailed thirty miles from the mountain when the crew heard *a fearful explosion* then witnessed a massive wave completely inundate the southern half of an island. A quarter of an hour later, the men were deluged with a downpour of mud, sand, and other debris they were unable to identify, which effectively encased their ship as in cement. Drawing near that fatal moment of the mountain's ultimate annihilation, the ship now seventy-five miles away, *the sky closed in,* the crew *enclosed in a darkness that might almost be felt,* the sky hanging *dark and heavy...Such darkness and such a time in general few would conceive and many...would disbelieve.* In those waters usually irradiated by the brutal blasts of the tropical sun, the darkness was so impenetrable that men were forced to grope their way along the deck. Though they shouted to one another in close physical proximity, they *could not see each other...the roaring of the volcano and the lightning from the volcano being something fearful.* Onto other ships fiery ashes fell, balls of fire striking decks and bursting into sparks, the copper sheathing of one rudder, set aglow by electrical discharges, shooting forth a shock so severe, a seaman's arm was paralyzed, ships swamped by volcanic ash *eight English thumbs deep,* one sailor in that utter darkness blindly walking off his deck, the barometric pressure dropping unimaginably low, the roar about them deafening. ⁵¹

The sea contributed its own horror as waves unrelated to the elegant swells of tides crashed and roared with demonic impetuosity, rising with alarming abruptness into monstrous crests before slamming down into inexplicably deep troughs. Terrified villagers pitifully climbed coconut trees to escape the raging sea as winds howled shrieking with hurricane force. The mountain continued to bellow as wickedly as the mountain in Milton's Hell, that *hill not far, whose grisly top / Belched fire,* the mighty plume of Krakatoa soaring upward over three times the height of Mount Everest. ⁵²

Also stranded in those waters was the excursion vessel, the 1,239 ton *Gouverneur-General Loudon,* which was filled to capacity with eighty-six passengers. Its captain, *T. H. Lindeman,* steered away from Krakatoa and made a desperate attempt to dock in Telok Betong, forty miles away, but the captain and his crew discovered that the three initial tsunamis had washed that harbor away. Understanding that the mountain had not yet been exhausted, and that tsunamis reach their greatest height near shore when they impact the continental shelf, he turned his ship around and headed out to the deep sea.

A series of three explosions followed by one almighty *crack of doom* heralded the death of the mountain, the final paroxysm, heard three thousand miles away, blasted debris far into the stratosphere, Krakatoa's death detonation at 10:02 a.m. issuing a shock wave which roared seven times around the world, causing millions to hear the planet itself utter a primal scream, and rocking buildings on their foundations five hundred miles away. Despite two days of terrors of biblical proportions, Krakatoa was still destined to bid history one final almighty adieux - a catastrophe which would claim the lives of thirty-six thousand people - one epic Himalayan tsunami worthy of the royal rhythms of Homer.

Amid a blinding storm of raining ash and pumice under daytime skies as black as pitch, the captain of the *Louden* ordered all passengers to descend into the hull. Displaying a supreme act of counter-intuition, he turned the ship toward the volcano, turned it to boldly face the volcano, and dropped both anchors in anticipation of what was about to come. Then abandoning all as worthless except raw courage and elemental compassion, the captain commanded his first mate to tie both of Lindeman's hands to the wheel of the ship. With a length of rope and the intricate interplay of knots and spokes, the captain of the *Louden* was tied to the wheel. T. H. Lindeman was now one with his ship. Then solemnly... patiently... he waited for the wave.

As the colossal wall of ebony water approached through the hellish darkness, the meager dimensions of the *Louden* began to slowly rise. Higher and higher at an ever-steeper angle of ascent, the *Louden* gradually drew near that monstrous crest. As the ship approached the summit of that watery Everest at a near vertical pitch, still the captain contended with the most horrific stress this planet can offer by solemnly remaining tied to his wheel. After that mighty crest had passed beneath them, the *Louden* slammed down upon the open sea with a primal scream, an epic impact which caused every board, every grain of timber, every bolt, and every nail to shudder with a mighty roar.

Not one passenger had perished. Not one crewman had died, because the captain, valuing only courage and compassion, had dared to face that exploding mountain, had dared to drop both anchors, and had dared to remain tied to his wheel. Everyone on the *Louden* survived the catastrophe of Krakatoa because Lindeman, the captain, had willed one thing – remaining steadfastly tied to his wheel, he dared to face the wave.

C8 80

146

Endnotes

Cover.
   Aeschylus. 'The Eumenides.' The Complete Greek
   Tragedies. David Grene, and Richmond Lattimore, eds.
   The Centennial Edition. Volume 1. Chicago: The University
   of Chicago Press, 1992. 169.

Pandemic of Opportunism.
   William Shakespeare. 'Julius Caesar.' The Tudor Edition of
   William Shakespeare: The Complete Works. Peter Alexander, ed.
   London: Collins, 1951. iv. 3. 218-219.

The Crisis.
   Aeschylus. 'The Libation Bearers.' Oresteia. Trans. Peter Meineck.
   Indianapolis: Hackett Publishing Company, Inc., 1998. 74.

The Physician as Defendant.
   Aeschylus. Agamemnon. Eduard Fraenkel, ed. Volume 1.
   Oxford: Clarendon Press, 1950. 119.

1. Thanos Viovolis, and Giorgos Zamboulakis. The Acoustical
   Mask of Greek Tragedy. Didaskalia. 19914-2015.
   ISSN 1321-4853.

   W. B. Standford. Greek Tragedy and the Emotions: An
   Introductory Study. New York: Routledge & Kegan Paul,
   Ltd., 1983.

The Patient or Loved One as Potential Plaintiff.
   Aeschyli. Eumenides. Trans. Bernard Drake.
   Cambridge: Macmillan and Co., 1853. 23.

2. Eric Berne, M. D. Games People Play: The Psychology of
   Human Relationships. The Book Press, 1964. 85.

3. Reginald Rose. <u>Twelve Angry Men</u>. Stage Version by Sherman L. Sergel. Woodstock: The Dramatic Publishing Company, MCMLXXIII. 10. 5.

4. Ibid., 15. 16.

5. Ibid., 5. 33. 34

Divine Abyss.
Christopher Pearse Cranch. 'So far, so near.'
<u>The Oxford Book of English Mystical Verse</u>. D. H. S. Nicholson, and A. H. E. Lee, eds. Oxford: Oxford University Press, 1962. 531-532.

6. Sophocles. <u>Antigone</u>. Angie Varakis, ed. Trans. Don Taylor. London: Metheun Drama, 2012. 21. 22.

7. Rudolf Otto. <u>The Idea of the Holy: An Inquiry into the Non-Rational Factor in the Idea of the Divine and its Relation to the Rational</u>. Trans. John W. Harvey. London: Oxford University Press, 1969. 5.

8. Ibid., 4. 12.

Aeschylus. 'The Eumenides.' Trans. Edith Hamilton. Line 183.

Kirk J. Schneider. <u>Horror and the Holy: Wisdom-Teachings of the Monster Tale</u>. Chicago: Open Court, 1993. 2.

Sarah Seymour-Winfield. <u>Images Old and New</u>. Dayton: Greyden Press, 2011. 18. 19.

Schneider. 11.

9. Walter F. Otto. <u>Dionysus: Myth and Cult</u>. Trans. Robert B. Palmer. Bloomington: Indiana University Press, 1965. 75. 201. 76.

Dylan Thomas. 'The Force that through the green fuse drives the flower.' The Collected Poems of Dylan Thomas. Daniel Jones, ed. New York: New Directions Books, 1957. 77.

Emily Dickinson. 'It is easy to work when the soul is at play –.' The Complete Poems of Emily Dickinson. Thomas H. Johnson, ed. Boston: Little, Brown and Company, 1960. 111.

10. Walter Otto. 136.

Rudolf Otto. 25.

The Trial of the Potential Plaintiff.
Meineck. 63.

11. Søren Kierkegaard. The Journals. Trans. Alexander Dru. A Kierkegaard Anthology. The Modern Library. Robert Bretall, ed. New York: Random House, 1946. 1.

12. William Shakespeare. 'A Comedy of Errors.' i. l. 14.

Aeschylus. 'The Eumenides.' Trans. Edith Hamilton. Line 183.

13. Alfred Lord Tennyson. 'In Memoriam.' D. H. S. Nicholson, and A. H. E. Lee, eds. 163.

Marcus Antonius. The New Dictionary of Thoughts: A Cyclopedia of Quotations. Tyron Edwards, C. N. Catrevas, and Jonathan Edwards, eds. New York: Standard Book Company, 1954. 194.

Robert Browning. 'Abt Vogler.' D. H. S. Nicholson, and A. H. E. Lee, eds. 192. 193.

Maeterlinck. Introduction to Ruysbroeck's *'L'Ornement des Noces Spirituelles.'* Mysticism. Evelyn Underhill. New York; Meridian, 1974. 340.

14. Ralph Harper. The Seventh Solitude: Metaphysical Homelessness in Kierkegaard, Dostoevsky and Nietzsche. Baltimore: The John Hopkins Press, 1967. 34. 36. 36.

15. John Milton. 'Paradise Lost. Book II.' The Poetical Works of John Milton. With Introduction by David Masson. New York: Thomas Y. Crowell & Co., 1892. 80.

Rudolf Otto. 15.

Psalm 42:7.

16. Richard Watson Dixon. 'Rapture; An Ode.' D. H. S. Nicholson, and A. H. E. Lee, eds. 275.

'The Scarlett Letter.' Mark Van Doren. Reprinted from The Scarlett Letter. Nathaniel Hawthorne. Philadelphia: Running Press, 1991. 201.

Toward a New Ontological Security.
Joseph Campbell. Creative Mythology: The Masks of God. New York: Penguin Group, 1968. 4.

17. G. C. Tympas. Carl Jung and Maximus the Confessor on Psychic Development: The Dynamics Between the 'Psychological' and the 'Spiritual'. New York: Routledge, 2014.

Ontological security refers to the 'confidence' that certain systems, such as physical   order and social norms, provide to individuals as well as to the feelings from and towards others, which generate self-identity in 'continuity' with the individuals' environments…(It) concerns continuity and trust in the external words, grounded in the feeling of security in the social order, a security that can further be understood as a mode of 'spiritual refuge.' 28-29.

Joseph Campbell. 4. 5.

18. William Shakespeare. 'King Lear.' iv. 6. 26.

Dionysius the Areopagite: 'The Mystical Theology.' Trans. Shine of Wisdom, Brook, Godalming. <u>Mysticism: A Study and an Anthology</u>. F. C. Happold, ed. Harmondsworth: Penguin Books, Ltd. 212. 213. 214.

19. Lev 24:20.

Aeschylus. 'The Eumenedes.' <u>The Oresteia</u>. Trans. Ted Hughes. New York: Farrar, Straus and Giroux, 1999. 181. 181. 181. 182.

20. Ibid., 189.

21. Ibid., 196. 196. 197. 198.

22. Aeschylus. 'The Eumenides.' Unknown translation. Line 750-751.

23. Aeschylus. 'The Eumenides.' Trans. Edith Hamilton. Line 179-183.

The Plaintiff's Grasp at Power.
Bertrand Russell. Tyron Edwards, C. N. Catrevas, and Jonathan Edwards, eds. 482.

Ego States.
Gen 4:8.

Games.
  Henry David Thoreau. 'Walden.'
  The Writings of Henry D. Thoreau: Walden. Princeton:
  Princeton University Press, 2004. 133.

24. Dylan Thomas. 'Fern Hill.' Daniel Jones, ed. 195 – 196.

25. Ibid., 196.

26. Paraphrase of Matt. 6:19-20.

  Matt. 19: 24. Mark 10: 25. Luke 18: 25.

27. Dylan Thomas. 'We have the fairy tales by heart.'
  Daniel Jones, ed. 59.

Entrances, Duration, and Aftermath.
  William Shakespeare. 'King John. ii. 1. 85. 'King Lear.' i. 1. 301.

Institutional Complicity.
  Donald Altman. The Mindfulness Code: Keys for Overcoming
  Stress, Anxiety, Fear, and Unhappiness. Novato: New World
  Library, 2010. 31. 56.

28. 'Dancing the Worlds. Susto (Fright) and Soul Loss.'
  http://www.dancingtheworlds.com

29. Ibid.

30. W. E. Vine. An Expository Dictionary of New Testament
  Words. Nashville: Royal Publishers, Inc., 1952.
  1180. 1144.

NAS Exhaustive Concordance of the Bible with Hebrew-
  Aramaic and Greek Dictionaries. The Lockman Foundation.

sunetos http://biblehub.com/greek 4908.htm
    dialogismos http://biblehub.com/greek 4908.htm

31. Ibid.

32. Ibid.

33. Ibid.

34. Arthur Miller. 'After the Fall.' I'm Ok – You're OK.
    Thomas A. Harris. New York: HarperCollins, 1969.
    141.

The Open and Loving Stance.
    Hippocrates. Hippocrates. G. P. Goold, ed.
    The Loeb Classical Library. Trans. W. H. S. Jones. Volumes I – IV.
    Cambridge: Harvard University Press, 1981. Vol. I. 319.

35. Mark 12: 31.

    Dr. Louis Lasagna. 'Nova.' Peter Tyson. pbs.org.

36. Thomas A. Harris. 234.

37. Paraphrase of endnote 35.

Hippocrates Today.
    Aeschylus. 'Prometheus Bound.' Trans. Edith Hamilton.
    Three Greek Plays: Prometheus Bound, Agamemnon,
    The Trojan Women. Trans. Edith Hamilton.
    New York: W. W. Norton & Company, 1965. 140.

38. Hippocrates. Vol I. 165.

39. Hippocrates. Vol II. 75. 115. Vol II. 121. Vol I. 89. Vol I. 287.

40. Hippocrates. Vol I. 321. Vol II. 217. Vol I. 27.

41. Hippocrates. Vol. II. 195.

42. Hippocrates. Vol. II. 201.

43. Hippocrates. Vol I. 313. Vol II. 203. 204. Vol I. 323.

44. Hippocrates. Vol. II. 227.

45. Hippocrates. Vol II. 203. 205. Vol. I. 313. 323. Vol II. 201.

46. Marcus Antonius. Tyron Edwards, C. N. Catrevas, and Jonathan Edwards, eds. 194.

    Robert Browning. 'Abt Vogler.' D. H. Nicholson, and A. H. E. Lee, eds. 193. 192.

    Maeterlinck. Introduction to Ruysbroeck's 'L'Ornement des Noces Spirituelles.' Underhill. 340.

August 27, 1883.
    Plutarch. Tyron Edwards, C. N. Catrevas, and Jonathan Edwards, eds. 105.

47. Edvard Munch. <u>Munch</u>. Jose Maria Faerna. New York: Harry N. Abrams, 1995. 16.

    Edvard Munch. <u>Edvard Munch: Behind the Scream</u>. Sue Prideaux. New Haven: Yale University Press, 2005.

48. Simon Winchester. <u>Krakatoa. The Day the World Exploded: August 27, 1883</u>. New York: HarperCollins Publishers Inc., 2003.

    The sound that was generated by the explosion of Krakatoa was enormous, almost certainly the greatest sound ever experienced by man on the face of the earth...Under the impact of Krakatoa's explosion,

thirteen percent of the earth's surface vibrated, and millions who lived there heard it, and when told what it was were amazed.
Winchester. 264.

49. From ship's log of Captain W. J. Watson. Winchester. 220.

50. From ship's log of Captain W. J. Watson. Winchester. 220 – 221.

51. From ship's log of Captain W. J. Watson. Winchester. 221 – 223.

52. John Milton. 'Paradise Lost. Book I.' 57.

CB ᘔ

Bibliography

Aeschylus. The Oresteia. Trans. Ted Hughes. The Eumenides. New York: Farrar, Straus and Giroux, 1999.

Aeschylus. Oresteia. Trans. Peter Meineck. Indianapolis: Hackett Publishing Company, Inc., 1998.

Alexander, Peter, ed. The Tudor Edition of William Shakespeare: The Complete Works. London: Collins, 1951.

Altman, Donald. The Mindfulness Code: Keys for Overcoming Stress, Anxiety, Fear, and Unhappiness. Novato: New World Library, 2010.

Aristotle. On Poetry and Style. Trans. G. M. A. Grube. Indianapolis: Bobbs-Merrill Company, Inc., 1958.

Berne, Eric, M. D. Games People Play: The Psychology of Human Relationships. The Book Press, 1964.

Bretall, Robert, ed. A Kierkegaard Anthology. The Modern Library. New York: Random House, 1946.

Campbell, Joseph. Creative Mythology: The Masks of God. New York: Penguin Group, 1968.

Dodge, Angela M., Ph.D., and Steven F. Fitzer, J.D. When Good Doctors Get Sued: A Practical Guide for Physicians Involved in Malpractice Lawsuits. Olawwa: Dodge & Associates, 200

Drake, Bernard. Aeschyli. Eumenedies. Trans. Bernard Drake. Cambridge: Macmillan and Co., 1853.

Tyron Edwards, C. N. Catrevas, and Jonathan Edwards, eds.
The New Dictionary of Thoughts: A Cyclopedia of Quotations.
New York: Standard Book Company, 1954.

Faerna, Jose Maria. Munch. New York: Harry N. Abrams, 1995.

Fraenkel, Eduard, ed. Aeschylus: Agamemnon. Trans. Eduard
Fraenkel. Volume I. London: Oxford University Press, 1950.

Grene, David, and Richmond Lattimore, ed. The Complete Greek
Tragedies. The Centennial Edition. Volume 1. Aeschylus. The
Eumenides. Chicago: The University of Chicago Press, 1992.

Hamilton, Edith. Three Greek Plays: Prometheus Bound,
Agamemnon, The Trojan Women. Trans. Edith Hamilton.
New York: W. W. Norton & Company, 1965.

Happold, F. C., ed. Mysticism: A Study and an Anthology.
Harmondsworth: Penguin Books, Ltd., 1970.

Harper, Ralph. The Seventh Solitude: Metaphysical Homelessness
in Kierkegaard, Dostoevsky and Nietzsche. Baltimore: The John
Hopkins Press, 1967.

Harris, Thomas A. I'm Ok – You're OK. New York: HarperCollins,
1969.

Hawthorn, Nathaniel. The Scarlett Letter. Philadelphia: Running
Press, 1991.

Goold, G. P. ed. Hippocrates. The Loeb Classical Library. Trans.
W. H. S. Jones. Volumes I – IV. Cambridge: Harvard University
Press, 1981.

James, John M., Ph. D., and W. Edward David, M. D. Physicians Survival Guide to Litigation Stress: Understanding, Managing, and Transcending a Malpractice Crisis. Layfayette: Physician Health Publications, L. L. C., 2006.

Johnson, Thomas H., ed. The Complete Poems of Emily Dickinson. Boston: Little, Brown and Company, 1960.

Jones, Daniel, ed. The Poems of Dylan Thomas. New York: New Directions Publishing Corporation, 1957.

Kerényi, Carl. Dionysus: Archetypal Image of Indestructible Life. Trans. Ralph Manheim. Bollingen Series LXV.2. Princeton: Princeton University Press, 1976.

Kierkegaard, Søren. Works of Love; Some Christian Reflections in the Form of Discourses. Trans. Howard and Edna Hong. New York: Harper Torchbooks, 1962.

---.Purity of Heart is to Will One Thing. Trans. Douglas V. Steere. New York: Harper Torchbooks, 1938.

Milton, John. The Poetical Works of John Milton. With Introductions by David Masson. New York: Thomas Y. Crowell & Co., 1892.

Nicholson, D. H. S., and A. H. E. Lee, eds. The Oxford Book of English Mystical Verse. London: Oxford University Press, 1962.

Nietzsche, Friedrich. The Birth of Tragedy and The Case Of Wagner. Trans. Walter Kaufmann. New York: Vantage Books, 1967.

Otto, Rudolf: <u>The Idea of the Holy: An Inquiry into the Non-Rational Factor in the Idea of the Divine and its Relation to the Rational</u>. Trans. John W. Harvey. London: Oxford University Press, 1969.

Otto, Walter F. <u>Dionysus: Myth and Cult</u>. Trans. Robert B. Palmer. Bloomington: Indiana University Press, 1965.

Rose, Reginald. <u>Twelve Angry Men</u>. Stage Version by Sherman L. Sergel. Woodstock: The Dramatic Publishing Company, MCMLXXIII.

Prideaux, Sue. <u>Edvard Munch: Behind the Scream</u>. New Haven: Yale University Press, 2005.

Schneider, Kirk J. <u>Horror and the Holy: Wisdom-Teachings of the Monster Tale</u>. Chicago: Open Court, 1993.

Seymour-Winfield, Sarah. <u>Images Old and New</u>. Dayton: Greyden Press, 2011.

Standford, W. B. <u>Greek Tragedy and the Emotions: An Introductory Study</u>. New York: Routledge & Kegan Paul Ltd., 1983.

Thoreau, Henry D. <u>The Writings of Henry D. Thoreau: Walden</u>. Princeton: Princeton University Press, 2004.

Tympas, G. C. <u>Carl Jung and Maximus the Confessor on Psychic Development: The Dynamics Between the 'Psychological' and the 'Spiritual'</u>. New York: Routledge, 2014.

Underhill, Evelyn. <u>Mysticism</u>. New York: Meridian, 1974.

Varakis, Angie, ed. <u>Antigone</u>. Sophocles. Trans. Don Taylor. London: Metheun Drama, 2010.

Vine, W. E. <u>An Expository Dictionary of New Testament Words</u>. Nashville: Royal Publishers, Inc., 1952.

Viovolis, Thanos, and Giorgos Zamboulakis. <u>The Acoustical Mask of Greek Tragedy</u>. Didaskalia, 1994-2015. ISSN 1321-4853.

Wiles, David. <u>Tragedy in Athens</u>. Cambridge: Cambridge University Press, 1997.

Winchester, Simon. <u>Krakatoa. The Day the World Exploded: August 27, 1883</u>. New York: HarperCollins Publishers Inc., 2003.

CB ED

Photo Acknowledgments

My gratitude to *Alamy Limited* and to *Shutterstock* for graciously
providing the color photographs throughout this book.

Alamy Limited.
6 – 8 West Central, 127 Olympic Avenue,
Milton Park, Abingdon Oxon, OX14 4SA
United Kingdom.

alamy.com

Shutterstock, Inc.
Empire State Building
350 Fifth Avenue, 21st Floor
New York, NY, 10118
USA.

shutterstock.com

Pandemic of Opportunism
Copyright: © Evlakhov Valeriy / Shutterstock Stock Photo

The Crisis
Copyright: © wavebreakermedia / Shutterstock Stock Photo

The Physician as Defendant
Copyright: © Stacey Newman / Shutterstock Stock Photo
Copyright: © Elgreko / Shutterstock Stock Photo
Copyright: © dominique landau / Shutterstock Stock Photo

The Patient or Loved One as Potential Plaintiff
Copyright: © Golden Pixeols LLC / Shutterstock Stock Photo

The Divine Abyss
Copyright: © ASE / Shutterstock Stock Photo

The Trial of the Potential Plaintiff
Copyright: © trekandshoot / Shutterstock Stock Photo

Toward a New Ontological Security
Copyright: © Susan E. Degginger / Alamy Stock Photo

April 4, 1968
Copyright: © PF-(usna) / Alamy Stock Photo

Part II

The Plaintiff's Grasp at Power
Copyright: © Maxx-Studio / Shutterstock Stock Photo

Ego States
Copyright © Monkey Business Images / Shutterstock Stock Photo

Games
Copyright © Monkey Business Images / Shutterstock Stock Photo

Entrances, Duration, Aftermath
Copyright © Barry Diomede / Alamy Stock Photo

Institutional Complicity
Copyright © Zurijeta / Shutterstock Stock Photo
Copyright © BPTU / Shutterstock Stock Photo
Copyright © Poylov Vladimir / Shutterstock Stock Photo

The Open and Loving Stance
Copyright © diazuoxin / Shutterstock Stock Photo

Hippocrates Today
Copyright © steve bly / Alamy Stock Photo

August 27, 1883
Copyright © Zoonar GmbH / Alamy Stock Photo

Cg 8O

www.ingramcontent.com/pod-product-compliance
Lightning Source LLC
Chambersburg PA
CBHW040126270326
41926CB00005B/86